Diana O'Donnell Moreno grew up in Torrance, California, near the beach cities of Hermosa and Redondo. After a long career in sales and marketing she turned to her first love, writing, to fill the void left by the loss of her husband. Diana currently resides in Las Vegas, Nevada and has two sons and five grandchildren living in California and Pennsylvania.

Dedicated to my one true love, my Louie, Luis Robert Moreno. You taught me so much in the twenty-six years we had together. I know you're popping the buttons off your heavenly wings as you see how far I have come since you left this world.

Diana O'Donnell Moreno

Lessons Learned from the Men I Have Loved & a Few I Loathe

AUSTIN MACAULEY PUBLISHERS™

LONDON • CAMBRIDGE • NEW YORK • SHARJAH

Ordering Information:
Quantity sales: special discounts are available on quantity purchases by corporations, associations, and others. For details, contact the publisher at the address below.

Publisher's Cataloging-in-Publication data
Moreno, Diana O'Donnell
Lessons Learned from the Men I Have Loved & a Few I Loathe

ISBN 9781645753919 (Paperback)
ISBN 9781645753926 (Hardback)
ISBN 9781645753933 (ePub e-book)

Library of Congress Control Number: 2020914252

www.austinmacauley.com/us

First Published (2020)
Austin Macauley Publishers LLC
40 Wall Street, 28th Floor
New York, NY 10005
USA

mail-usa@austinmacauley.com
+1 (646) 5125767

Table of Contents

Foreword

The constantly twisting and turning road we call Life, begins the moment we draw our first breath, scream our arrival or quietly open our eyes. Climb steep hills or tumble head first into deep valleys. Choose a path at crossroads and forks in the road. Make decisions that leave us feeling brave or cowardly. The choice is ours. No one else can ultimately make it for us. Influence yes, decide no. When you make your choice, dear reader, and the end result is not what you'd hoped, you can learn from the experience. To embrace change or wallow in self-pity. Yes, the choice is ours.

For me, I choose to embrace new experiences. Some are fabulously wonderful. Others, not so much. But above all, I have *learned* from each experience. First as a sweet, wide-eyed, innocent-as-the-day-is-long child, then as a slightly-on-the-wild-side, I-know-everything teenager, later as a forced-to-mature-way-too-soon young adult, and finally, at this stage of my life, an I-may-be-old-but-I-refuse-to-act-it senior citizen.

Growing up in a household of mostly women, which included my mother and two sisters—one younger and one older—the only daily exposure I had to the male gender was my father. Although I loved my mom and sisters, I have always been drawn to men. Men are my favorite gender because of their machismo. Maleness. Instructions-are-to-be-used-only-as-a-last-resort attitude. Ah yes, men are my weakness and this book is filled with lessons learned from the over two hundred men I have known and admired during my years on this planet. My dad. Two husbands—one I divorced and the other whose life ended far too soon. My two sons, and their sons. Men I have worked with and for, and men I have had mad crushes on, dated, and/or slept with. The lessons are real, based on facts that I may or may not have taken certain literary liberties to enhance or minimize. Some names have been changed to protect the innocent, as well as those guilty of hurting me either intentionally or unintentionally, and, of course, to prevent lawsuits.

To the men who have traveled in and out of my life, see if you can find yourselves amongst the pages of my book. Do not be offended if you didn't make the grade … this time. Perhaps you will in my next book if you were (or are) wonderfully or tragically memorable enough.

To my readers, feel free to use my book any way you wish—as a delightful reminder of the fun you've had in your own life or to live vicariously through my escapades. Or use my lessons as fodder for provocative discussions with your friends. If you are easily offended by risqué behavior, you may wish to forego reading, as it is deliciously naughty, but then again it might be just what the doctor ordered to add a little spice to your life.

So, grab your favorite beverage, kick off your shoes, and get ready to laugh, cry, and—hopefully—be thoroughly entertained by *Lessons Learned from the Men I Have Loved & a Few I Loathe.*

Chapter 1. Daddy's Girl

I came into this world kicking and screaming, the middle child of three daughters born to a lower middle-class family living on the poor side of town near the beach cities in Los Angeles County, California.

Mama was feisty at five foot one *and a half* inches tall (don't forget that half inch), weighing in at just shy of a hundred pounds. Her baby-fine, stick-straight auburn hair was permed and bobby-pin-dried into tight curls, as was the fashion at that time. Creamy ivory skin provided the perfect backdrop for her big, ocean-blue eyes. With a gorgeous to-die-for figure of full breasts, tiny waist, firm round hips, and shapely petite legs, she was unknowingly the envy of her peers and the object of desire to many a man, young and old alike, and at the age of fourteen, she was already engaged to a local boy. That is, until Daddy came into the picture. Oh yeah, my daddy was a sight to behold, a force to be reckoned with, a soldier in uniform.

Mama and Daddy met at Banning Park in Wilmington, California during the tumultuous years of World War II. After the bombing of Pearl Harbor, Banning Park was commandeered as an Army base to protect the Port of Los Angeles in nearby San Pedro. Many a young girl envisioned meeting and marrying a heroic soldier, including my tiny mama and her tall, blonde friend, Trudy. After school one Friday afternoon, under a bluer-than-blue sky, the teenaged girls decided the time was right and crossed the street to walk through the park. They paused occasionally to bolster their courage. Choosing the playground swings to exhibit some sense of nonchalance, they settled in the wide strips of black leather that served as seats and, with their feet barely reaching the sand beneath them, slowly swung back and forth, hoping a handsome soldier would notice and give them a push. Oh, to feel a man's hands on their bodies must have seemed like an unattainable fantasy.

Ladies' man that he was, Daddy immediately spotted the girls and got his friend Smitty's attention by nodding toward the swings. Little did my daddy know he would soon fall in love with the auburn-haired pixie perched on the swing. All he knew was that his five-foot-ten, one-hundred-sixty-pound, tightly muscled body was suddenly reduced to a spineless jelly fish at the sight of the pint-sized beauty. Daddy's light brown crew cut hair, although styled with pomade in an attempt to tame its unruliness, nearly stood on end as his hazel green eyes grew wide with unexpected pleasure. He stood behind Mama and slowly began to push her. "My name's Frank, what's yours, sweetheart?" Mama answered sweetly, "Wanda. My name's Wanda." Dark haired, good-looking Smitty introduced himself to Trudy but there was no spark. It was Mama and Daddy's time. Mama was so entranced by the dashing young man that she invited him to Sunday dinner with the family, and thus began a romance that lasted over fifty years.

Frank and Wanda were married on June 24, 1943 and spent one night together before Daddy was transferred to

Washington State. Grandma told Mama to be brave on her wedding night because she would be forced to endure terrible, hurtful things, but to close her eyes, lay still and it would soon be over. That night, out of sheer terror, Mama locked herself in the bathroom of the tiny motel room and refused to come out. Daddy had just one precious night to make love to his beautiful young wife so he pleaded and coaxed, finally promising he would never hurt her. At long last, she unlocked the door and peered nervously at him with fearful red-rimmed eyes. True to his word, he was gentle and sweet, and Mama was shocked that it just hurt a little at first and then oh-my-goodness-how-can-I-feel-this-way amazing!

During a short leave a few months later, their lovemaking created my sister Linda. Soon the war ended and Daddy returned to his joyful wife and skeptical young daughter. At just over a year-old, Linda had no idea who this strange man was and her terrified screams could be heard up and down the street every time he came near her or his wife. After hours of Mama nursing and rocking and singing softly to her, the exhausted infant fell soundly asleep. Daddy at long last climbed into his wife's bed and held her tightly in his arms, rejoicing the war was over and that at long last their life as a couple could begin free of uncertainty and chaos.

By late 1948, life was as purely wonderful as a life could be for the young couple. Their daughter had grown into an adorable, blonde haired, hazel-eyed precious four-year-old and Daddy had a good paying union job at a local oil refinery. A lush green lawn and budding rose bushes on either side of the front door shouted to the world proud ownership of a brand new, white picket-fenced, two-bedroom, one-bath tract home with a low interest, no down payment G.I. loan. Unfortunately, once the harsh reality of a post-war economy set in, their seemingly perfect world crumbled like a poorly built fence during a ninety mile an hour windstorm. Daddy's union went out on strike, he was out of work, and Mama was eight months pregnant with me.

My birth became a joyous burden to the idealistic young couple. Daddy proudly picketed with his fellow union members, shouting encouragement to each other as they held their signs high while jeering at the "scabs" crossing the line. Each worker was convinced he was protecting the entire American workforce from the greed of big business. Mama stayed home with us kids, taking in ironing from the wealthier families for a few dollars a week and watching anxiously as the bills quickly piled up. Each night the men returned home from the picket line assuring their families that the strike would be over any day, we just have to be patient. The days grew into weeks, weeks into months, and still no end in sight.

One by one, the picketers were forced to abandon their posts to look for work, taking non-union jobs just to keep roofs over their heads and food on the tables for the wives and kids. Reluctantly, Daddy left the picket line and took a job laying asphalt for a contractor, paving parking lots for the post-war building boom of apartment buildings, offices, and shopping centers. It was a backbreakingly hard, miserable job during the hot, dry months of summer. But the winters were worse.

A harsh, rainy winter could put us in the poorhouse for sure, because you can't lay hot asphalt during a rainstorm.

No work meant no paycheck, sometimes for weeks. Never knowing if winter would be dry and prosperous or wet and miserable, Mama learned to save every extra cent in an empty apple butter jar—cleverly shaped like an apple with a stem and leaf—that she kept hidden on the floor of her closet quite literally "for a rainy day." Daddy tried hard to fill the gaps in his income by doing odd jobs. Temporary workers were paid in cash at the end of each day so he'd stop and pick up a few groceries and maybe a penny candy for us kids on his drive home. As was the custom, back when neighbors actually knew each other and the community truly cared about its members, anonymous friends would leave a bag of groceries on the kitchen table while we were at church (no one locked their doors back then). That's how we got through the really tough times.

To me, it seemed all men must be like my complex daddy. One day, a benevolent, laughing god bursting through the door with a magical pink box filled with sweet treats from the bakery when times were good. Then a mean-spirited demon during the rainy season, drinking and loudly bemoaning the fact that there just wasn't any work to be had when the skies opened up and the rain poured down. "Can I control the weather?" he would mutter. "Hell no!" He'd light another cigarette, take a swig from his beer bottle, burp loudly for emphasis while wiping the dribble off his chin with the back of his calloused hand.

As a good little girl, I did everything I could to put a smile on my daddy's face. During the summer when the winds were warm, the skies were blue and Mama's flowerbeds were filled with bright purple pansies, fragrant pink carnations, and cobalt blue bachelor buttons, I'd dance a silly dance in the green grass of our front yard. The dance always began by me ceremoniously picking a flower and tucking it behind one of Daddy's ears. I'd fling my arms high in the air, skip to and fro, shaking my body back and forth while rolling my eyes at him. To see a smile light up his sun parched, worry-lined face made all my antics worthwhile. I became his favorite, little ole chubby me, and he'd sing, "Roly-Poly, Daddy's Little Fatty," to me. I was in heaven. Daddy didn't sing special songs to my sisters, so I must be his favorite!

One day, the uncertainty of construction work became too much to tolerate. Daddy swallowed his pride, drove downtown, and applied for a job with the City, and then waited. And waited. Each day he checked the mailbox. Tore open letters from banks offering free toasters to anyone opening a new account. A bill from the water company. A Past-due notice from the electric company, and another from Sears and Roebuck threatening to repossess the brand-new refrigerator bought on credit last year when things were good. A letter to Mama from Aunt Ophelia in Wilmington and a postcard from Cousin Alfie vacationing in Toledo, Ohio. But nothing from the City.

Every time the phone rang, he sprang out of his chair and anxiously ran to answer it. "Honey, it's your Aunt Geraldine," he'd dejectedly announce. Then Susie from down the street called to ask us to be on the lookout for her dog Old Blue because he'd jumped the fence and was running the streets again. The school called to report a chickenpox epidemic at a nearby school and to keep an eye out for blisters on us kids.

Ten days go by and finally, hallelujah, a letter of congratulations arrived in the mail. My daddy, my hero, the first man I ever loved, the man who would love me forever because I always put a smile on his face, was the City of Torrance, California's newest refuse collector (a.k.a. trash man), with a steady pay check and benefits.

Lesson 1: Put a smile on a man's face and he will love you forever.

Chapter 2. What Roy Rogers Didn't Tell Me

When I was growing up, cowboy movies and television shows were my very favorite form of entertainment. John Wayne and Gene Autry were my heroes as I watched them rescue damsels in distress and shoot evil villains. But my favorite scenes involved the hero jumping off a building onto his waiting horse. Be still my beating heart!

So, as an adventurous, *very* independent five-year-old, my curiosity got the best of me one bright, summer day. I decided it was time to try some of this cowboy stuff myself. I donned my brown felt cowboy hat and tied the strings under my chin to ensure it would remain securely on my head. I jauntily buckled my leather holster around my chubby little waist and carefully placed my cold metal toy gun in its holster, patting it to make sure it was secure. I wiggled my feet into my getting-to-be-too-small scuffed leather cowboy boots. Checking in the mirror to assure myself I looked like an authentic cowboy, I pulled the cap pistol from its holster, whirled around, and pointed it at my image in the mirror, then twirled it. Unlike my movie heroes, I dropped it, but I picked it up, shoved it confidently back in the holster, nodded in satisfaction at myself in the mirror, and headed out to the lonesome prairie, my backyard.

I surveyed the area for the best possible location. First thing I saw was a green lawn with two steel poles strung with four clotheslines and a handmade clothespin holder made out of a flour sack hanging on the far end. Mama had just hung out our bed sheets to dry, to give them that "fresh outdoor smell," but I think mostly so the afternoon ocean breeze could remove the wrinkles pressed in by the hand-operated washing machine wringer. Nope, better stay far away from those sheets. Mama would skin me alive if I was to get them dirty.

Off to the right was a fruit tree, branches heavy with plump, ripening apricots whose branches might come in handy to hang a wily varmint caught trying to steal any of the cattle lowing in the distance of my imagination. Further back was a summer garden crowded with low-lying vines of squash and watermelon, wooden trellises heavy with green beans and boysenberries, and two rows of green stalks loaded with ripening cobs of golden corn. Nope—fruits and vegetables could not fulfill my cowboy aspirations, but maybe my imaginary cattle drive cook, Lefty, could do something with 'em. I pictured Lefty as a gray-haired, cranky old man with a wild look in one eye and a big, bushy salt-and-pepper beard on his sunburnt face, too old and lame to herd cattle any more. But he could turn even the stringiest, meagerest, most pitiful of ingredients into a veritable prairie feast we called cowboy stew.

As I continue to scrutinize the prairie, my gaze rests on the covered patio made out of discarded World War II airplane glass. Now that would be a mighty fine jail for criminals should I choose to become the sheriff of the small, make-believe town I call Dusty, for the clouds of dirt my pony kicks up as we race down Main Street. Then my eyes widen as they spot two weather-beaten wooden sheds standing side by side, each over seven feet high. One housed the vegetables and jellies Mama preserved in clear glass mason jars but the other—ah the other, was filled with my dad's tools and definitely, certainly, by cracky, looked like the best candidate to fulfill my ultimate cowboy fantasy.

Inside the tool shed, a sawhorse that most certainly resembled a *real* horse beckoned to me. Out I pulled it into the warm afternoon sunshine, carefully maneuvering it until indeed it was the perfect distance away from the shed. Piling three wooden crates one upon the other proved to be a little more daunting than I anticipated. With the determination of a very willful child, however, all obstacles were overcome and the crudely built ladder was ready to be mounted by me, a tiny cowboy with bouncing blonde curls and bright blue eyes.

Oh, so carefully I ascend the unsteady, makeshift "steps," steadying myself by resting my right foot on the red painted wooden fence adjacent to the shed. I take a deep breath and take that last giant step from the fence to the roof of the shed. There I am, standing tall and proud on the shed's tin roof, looking down what seemed a *really* long way at my faithful sawhorse steed, affectionately named Buttercup. Buttercup nickered softly in my mind as she waited patiently for me to make my much-anticipated descent. With my cowboy hat waving mightily in one hand, I loudly exclaim, "Hi-Ho, Buttercup, and away we go." Down I went, jumping to an absolutely perfect landing!

Except, the excruciating pain was more than my young body could take. I immediately blacked out and fell off Buttercup into a tiny heap on the hard adobe ground.

The next thing I remember is my older sister, Linda, hovering over me, crying and screaming, "Mama, come quick! I think Diana finally went and killed herself." White as a sheet with blood oozing down my legs, I was carried into the house. Now, in those days, we weren't sissies. We didn't go to the doctor's unless bones were at an obviously gross angle. Or sticking out of your flesh. Or the bleeding could not be stopped. Or pus was nastily oozing from an open wound. Nope, first aid was administered at home. After peeling off my clothes and giving me a gentle sponge bath to remove the sticky, drying blood, a careful examination of my entire body was made. Mama concluded that although some bruises were beginning to appear and there were a few scratches, all bones appeared intact. The impact when I straddled the sawhorse had, apparently, broken my hymen and that's where the majority of the blood came from.

Since a trip to the hospital was not warranted, I spent the day propped up in bed amongst fluffy pillows, surrounded by my favorite stuffed teddy bears and baby dolls with eyes that closed and limbs that moved. Ice was applied to my nether region, to bring down the swelling of my heavily bruised lady parts, and my very favorite comfort food lunch was brought to me *in bed* on a beautiful silver serving tray normally reserved for holidays only. It held two slices of Oscar Mayer bologna on unbelievably soft Wonder bread heavily spread with Best Foods mayonnaise, and cut on the bias in quarters creating dainty triangles. A cup of

Campbell's, oh-so-creamy, cream of tomato soup in its own Campbell's mug and an ice-cold glass of milk sat next to the sandwich. Finishing off this veritable feast was a still-warm-from-the-oven, oh-so-delicious, giant chocolate chip cookie.

While I solemnly consumed my lunch, Mama gently explained to me that movies and T.V. shows are not real. They're make-believe and the stunts were done by stuntmen, trained adults. Not five-year-old little girls. Needless to say, I learned my lesson and from then on left the cowboy stuff to the professionals.

Years later, when arthritis set in, X-rays revealed that my poor little tailbone had been snapped off by the fall and was hanging on by the spinal cord. Even if Mama had taken me to the doctors, they couldn't have done anything. Not then and not even today. I was cautioned to never squarely land on my tush again, because I could sever the spinal cord, which is—I'm just guessing here—not a good thing. The lack of a hymen meant my first sexual encounter was a little less painful than normal and involved no blood at all, so hooray for that.

Lesson 2: Leave the cowboy stunts to trained professionals.

Chapter 3. A Man in Uniform

At the tender age of thirteen, my very best girlfriend, Lenore, and I ditched school one sunny, cloudless fall morning and walked a whole mile to the nearby shoreline of the South Bay, where we buried our toes in the warm sand and watched as the beautiful white-capped waves crashed, sending water higher and higher toward us. When the cold ocean water reached our bare toes, we ran screaming up the beach like the little girls we were, catching the attention of a twenty-something out-of-work beach bum. "Well, hello there, girls. I'm Dave," he said. "What are you doing out of school?" We solemnly explained that we were high school dropouts, old enough to do whatever we wanted. Dave invited us to leave our shoes on his beach towel and play Frisbee with him. By the end of the morning, Lenore and I felt like we had been friends with Dave forever—even though his long, sun bleached hair, romantically full lips, perfect unblemished face, and bronzed muscular body in loose Hawaiian swim trunks screamed "forbidden fruit!"

Later in the afternoon, Lenore discreetly went off to use the restroom and left me alone with Dave. He took the opportunity to cradle me gently in his arms, tell me what a beautiful young woman I was becoming as he bent down slowly to softly kiss my eager lips.

Wow! For the very first time in my life, I felt like a *woman* as he held me in his strong, bronzed arms and taught me how to kiss, not just a peck like boys had kissed me before. Oh no. His lips kissed mine for a long time. Then I felt him gently push his tongue past my lips. For what seemed like an eternity, he caressed my tongue with his, transporting me to another level of consciousness before he slowly pulled away. I was fascinated by how good the kiss felt and this new, tingly sensation between my legs. I wanted to keep going but he was wise enough to stop. He looked deep into my eyes, thanked me for a lovely day, and walked away.

Lenore passed by him on her way back from the restroom and asked me why he was muttering something about "She might *look* like a woman, but she's just a baby in disguise" and he "was not going to be tricked into another statutory rape affair." Her eyes grew wide as I told her about our wonderfully fabulous kissing, leaving out the part about the strange twitching I felt in his trunks as he held me close and the tingling sensation between my own thighs. After washing our feet and putting our shoes back on, we began the long trek back to school. Neither one of us would ever quite be the same as we walked back onto campus in time to hear the final school bell ring and watch as the laughing, shouting kids streamed out of their classrooms, heading home for the day.

The encounter with Dave intrigued me. I need to know more about the kissing and holding thing and the endless possibilities that a male-female relationship could lead to and an assessment of my body. I eagerly remove my clothing and impartially study my image in the full-length mirror hanging on the back of the bedroom door. My face has elongated from chubby cheeks to a wholesome, natural beauty with blue eyes that change with my mood. The curly blonde hair on my head and down *there* made me blush just a little. My scrutiny revealed a very curvaceous body with small breasts and waist, full shapely hips, and long lovely legs. Not bad, I thought to myself. Actually, damn near perfect. I was delighted to discover it was true what this man, Dave, had told me—I *am* rapidly becoming a woman. It is definitely time to put away childish things and truly embrace my womanhood. I must start dressing more like a teenager than a child! A few months later, I innocently attend a church pajama party and sure enough, fall in puppy love with a nineteen-year-old young man.

I'd been attending the church for a couple of years as a child. But now I am a woman—after all, I had been kissed, by a *man*. So in preparation for the Saturday night party, I carefully coif my blonde hair into two cute little pigtails, place Porky Pig hair clips on both sides of my head, accent my blue eyes with a pale, creamy blue eye shadow and dark brown mascara, finishing my mature look with an oh-so-barely-pink lipstick. I chastely dress in Sylvester and Tweety Bird cotton pj's, but before entering the church hall roll up the elbow length sleeves and past-the-knee pants and open the top button of the blouse so the swell of my breasts could peek out just a tiny bit.

I arrive at the party fully convinced I am ready to be in a *relationship*. I glance around the room slowly until my attention is drawn to a tall, muscular young man with jet-black hair slicked back into a ducktail. He's holding a pink plastic baby pacifier between his perfect white teeth and a pale blue baby bonnet on his head is neatly tied with a jaunty bow. His tight white t-shirt sports a sexy pack of Marlboros rolled in one sleeve, and the form-fitting shirt is tucked into his even tighter Levi's, cuffed just enough to show off polished black loafers and bright white socks. Oh yes, he is mighty fine and he's walking toward me!!!

He introduces himself as Bill and asks if he could sit with me. Once I shyly agree, he looks across the room and gives a chin up signal to the friend he had arrived with, a silent message to "Stay away because I got me a girl." I soon learn he is five years older than me, graduated from a rival high school two years earlier, just received his certificate from a trade school, and is working as a printer's apprentice. Bingo, home run! This guy has not just one but *two* diplomas, a good paying job, and—for the cherry on top— he flat-out owns a car! Not just a car. A totally bitchin' red with white trim, 1955 Dodge two-door hardtop Coronet with a 271 cubic-inch V8 engine *and* automatic tranny! Be still my heart, this guy is every girl's dream come true.

Soon the party begins and we join in the festivities, first trying to outdo each other in a baby bottle drinking contest (man, those things are hard to suck!!!), then a Bible quiz (I win of course), and, finally, the sack race. Bill and I win, beating the closest couple by taking a giant leap just before reaching the finish line, causing us to fall on our faces and laugh out loud until we are both totally and completely out of breath. As the evening wears on, we talk and laugh and talk some more while drinking sparkling red fruit punch and eating vanilla cupcakes topped with butter cream frosting and lots of fun multi-colored sprinkles until the party ends far too soon, at ten o'clock.

Bill asks if he could escort me outside to wait for my parents, and I readily agree. We held hands as we walked together. Once outside, he takes me in his arms, looks deeply into my eyes, and was about to say something when we both jumped a mile at the sound of Daddy's horn honking when he caught us in the glare of his headlights. I giggle childishly as I climb in the car and turn around just in time to see Bill waving goodbye. I return the wave and sigh deeply as I watch him grow smaller and smaller as we drive away. Daddy asked who the young man is and I tell him he is the dreamiest boy I've ever met. Daddy tells me to behave myself and not get in any trouble with this boy. Trouble? What kind of trouble, I wonder?

To my utter amazement, Bill attends my church the next day, hoping to find me. I swear I almost swooned. This handsome boy likes me! He really, really, *really* likes me enough to come to Sunday school in hopes of seeing me again! And so, my first relationship began. We date throughout my teen years, during which he taught me how to French kiss with our lips touching and tongues tangled together, how it feels to have my breasts touched, what a grown man's body looks like "down there," and the miracle that happens when it gets excited while we neck and pet.

Go ahead ladies, fan yourselves, this was pretty hot stuff for a young teenager.

Oh my, my, the supreme power I now hold over making his body react to my touch. It's exciting and absolutely intoxicating. Until one night, we're engaged in a very heated necking session at the town's pitch-black lover's lane when our passion screeched to a halt under the brightest, harshest light I have ever seen. Perhaps it's a UFO? No such luck. I would have rather been abducted by aliens than seeing that cop holding his flashlight on our half-naked bodies, eyes bulging with the terrified look of very guilty teenagers. He growls at us, "Get dressed, for God's sake, and you, Missy, step out of the car."

Officer Muldoon is a middle-aged, stout little man with a receding hairline obvious even under his police cap. He has a heavy five o'clock shadow, a big nose, and beady little eyes. Then he insists he recognizes me from previous encounters and is certain he has taken me to jail before, which he most definitely had *not*.

As the seemingly inevitable future of newspaper headlines branding me a slut—"LOCAL TEENAGE GIRL CAUGHT WITH HER PANTIES DOWN"—and my boyfriend going on trial for statutory rape—"LOCAL PRINTER'S APPRENTICE ARRESTED FOR INDECENT EXPOSURE AND FONDLING OF NOT-SO-SWEET HIGH SCHOOL GIRL"—flashed before my eyes, I gently place my warm hand on the officer's arm, look into his tiny, twitching eyes with my best Bambi expression, and begin to spin a very tall tale to get us out of this mess. Now, as you may recall, my Daddy is a garbage man, but that is not how I tell it.

"How are you, Officer Muldoon? As you may recall, Father is with the city," I politely explain in a haughty voice after I'd noticed the gold wedding band on his left ring finger and the name on his badge. "He and I attended the Police Department's Christmas party last year where we met you and your delightful wife just before dinner was served. What was it they served that night? We attended so many dinner parties this past holiday season." I glance down, hoping he had taken the bait.

Muldoon quickly answers, "Romaine lettuce with tiny little tomatoes and fancy cut radishes, Cornish game hen with the best au gratin potatoes I have ever eaten. And with steamed asparagus and hollandaise sauce—in December no less! That must have cost the city a pretty penny. Oh yeah, and chocolate mousse, I think that's what it's called, for dessert."

Shaking my head in agreement, I said, "Of course, now I remember. By the way, how is your lovely spouse?"

Muldoon's face and tone soften as he replies, "She's feeling better. Turned out to be just a bad cold but she's fine now."

"Give her my best, please?" I reply.

Oh, *all* of it is a lie, but I was ever so earnest as I continue to gaze directly into his piercing little eyes. After a moment of mentally analyzing the facts as relayed by me, Officer Muldoon glanced over at Bill's stricken face, then back at me and delivers his decision. "That's right," Muldoon exclaims as his brow furrows and his tiny eyes grow wide with perceived recognition. "Your pop's our new city councilman, right?"

I smile and nod while he apologizes profusely for spoiling our evening, then holds the passenger car door open for me to get back in. As he closes the door, he asks me to please not tell my father that he had bothered us. Standing straight and tall, he signals for us to drive away, and I watched out the back window until I see him get back in his police car and pull away in the opposite direction. I can finally breathe again.

"Man, oh man. That was some fancy footwork you did back there," Bill says. "How do you come up with that stuff?"

I throw my head back and laugh. "Made all of it up. He asked me not to tell Daddy!!! Are you kidding? I want to live to see another day, don't you?"

So, Bill drives me straight home. I sit way over on the passenger side with my hands clasped tightly in my own lap instead of in his. He walks me to the front door (twenty minutes before my curfew of midnight, mind you) and kisses me on the cheek. We never again spoke of the incident *or* parked in Lover's lane.

But the lesson I learned that night served me well over the years whenever I found myself in a situation that needed, shall we say, a little embellishment of the facts.

Lesson 3: A man will believe anything if you say it with a sincere smile on your face and a warm hand on his arm.

Chapter 4. Bye-Bye, Bill!

Soon after that dreadful night on lover's lane, my slightly-on-the-arrogant-side boyfriend, Bill, was drafted into the army and whisked off to boot camp. Six long weeks of countless fantasies lay before me as I envisioned our life together as a military family.

First the wedding, where he would stand proudly in our church, filled with white roses surrounded by the sweetest of baby's breath and the tiniest of green palm fronds. Bill wearing his dress uniform, hat jauntily cocked a tiny bit to one side, just like my daddy wore his. Flower girls tossing lavender rose petals onto the long aisle's polished wooden floor. Bridesmaids dressed in the palest, lavender-iest, beautiful-est taffeta dresses the world had ever seen, walking majestically before me. Tears would fill my husband-to-be's eyes when he saw me walk down the aisle in a pure white wedding gown covered in lace and pearls, white petticoat peeking out just above white satin slippers, long lacy veil demurely covering my face.

Family and friends would hold their collective breath as Bill and I read our handwritten vows, pledging to love one another forever and ever, in sickness and health, through rain and sleet and dead of night, until death pried his dead hand out of mine. (*Hey, it's my fantasy, I can include anything I want in our vows*.) We would spend a perfect honeymoon in perfect Hawaii. In a perfect hotel room, returning to our perfect home filled with one dog, two cats, a parakeet, and a bowl with seven perfect goldfish, all of which dance gleefully at our return. Except for the goldfish. They swim gleefully, blowing underwater bubbles. Here we will spend the rest of our lives in a perfect neighborhood, raising perfect children. Our families proudly attending countless military ceremonies where Bill would receive medal after medal for bravery and other military stuff, even managing to end the Vietnam conflict, later winning the Cold War single-handedly. Bill retiring after thirty years in the military, to enjoy our lives together as perfect grandparents to perfect grandchildren.

My entire life lay before me and I would be the very best army wife and army kids' mother to the very best career soldier ever. Oh yes, it was so very clear what path I was meant to travel in this wonderful, opportunity filled thing we call Life.

But wait, what's this? A phone call from Bill. Boot camp doesn't allow phone calls! Is someone pulling a prank on me? Nope, it's him. He was kicked out, labeled "failure to adapt," and was being, shamefully, sent home. The drill sergeant discovered that, despite his best efforts to corral Bill's willful behavior, he simply could not obey an order, even questioning why he could not wake up at his usual time, 12-noon. Bill's absolute and total failure at an attempted military career did not sit well with my father, who was a proud WWII army veteran, and I'm sure you can imagine his utter and complete disgust for this young man.

My own personal sense of ethics and utter disappointment at how Bill had ruined *my* life and *my* aspirations and *my* fantasies as a military wife would no longer allow me to date this unadaptable young man. I callously told him I was ashamed of his expulsion from the army and instructed him to "Never darken my door again." I seem to recall closing my eyes and placing the back of my hand against my forehead for added emphasis. But perhaps an aging memory has embellished upon the actual facts, although it does make for a rather dramatic end to my first romance, does it not?

But I digress. Back to the story: my dreams of a military wedding, attending medal ceremonies, raising our children on military bases, seeing the world at Uncle Sam's expense, enjoying the camaraderie of sister military wives—the dreams suddenly and irrevocably vanished. This poor young man had just been tossed aside by his country like a used condom, who now was being crushed beneath the heel of his long-time girl, called for days begging me to take him back. But no, my bruised ego would not allow me to give my heart to a malcontent. Eventually the phone calls stopped. Four months later, I heard from a mutual friend Bill had married an older, divorced woman with a bunch of snot-nosed kids and moved to Canada. Canada!!! The news that he had forsaken his country was shocking, but how had he gotten over *me* so *quickly*? Our puppy love affair had lasted three years—my whole life as a teenager—but why should I care? He was, at least by my standards, a born loser.

Perhaps because of my father, I am still drawn to military veterans because of their strength of character and determination in the face of adversity. They're heroes to me.

I mean, after all they passed boot camp, didn't they? I admire and thank each and every veteran for their service and loyalty to our country, and am disappointed in men my age who either dodged the draft or failed the physical exam. (Picture me waving a tiny red, white, and blue United States of America flag while belting out a slightly out-of-tune God Bless America. Yep, that's me. Patriotic as the day is long. Don't like it? Too bad.)

A few decades later, I understood that not everyone is physically or mentally suited to serve their country and was far better off supporting the war effort back home in the States. After all, with most of the nation's young men deployed overseas, we needed *some* boys left behind to take us girls out on Saturday night, right?

Lesson 4: Soldiers know how to follow orders—after all, they passed boot camp.

Chapter 5. And Along Comes Bob

So, exit stage left (actually Canada) Boyfriend #1, with his new wife and step-kids, and enter into my never-to-be-dull life the new kid in school. Bob was a good looking, sweet teenager from Denver, Colorado who always arrived at our first-period class early, standing patiently outside the door for school to begin. You know the type: dark brown hair parted carefully on the right, both sides slicked back and the front combed up and over kind of like an ocean's wave. Crisp white short-sleeved dress shirt, complete with a white plastic pocket-protector filled with pencils, pens, and a protractor (do they still use them in school, I wonder?). In other words, a total and complete nerd. Now, my first thought was "This guy needs a life," but I gradually began arriving earlier so I could talk to him. He had an easy laugh that made his brown eyes crinkle closed and a guileless good-heartedness that was danged appealing. Who knew it could happen? I was totally smitten by a boy-next-door kinda guy.

It's now the end of my senior year, Bill was out of my life forever, and I was desperately hoping Bob would ask me out. But no such luck. Graduation comes and goes. I pick up my diploma on the last day of school and still *no* sign of interest from Bob in taking our friendship to the next level, dating. I tearfully clear out my senior locker, wish my friends good luck in their next life, and meet my annoying younger sister Wilma at my car—a 1953 Chrysler Imperial with automatic transmission, electric windows and seats, that I affectionately (and appropriately, my teenage mind insisted) named the Pimpmobile for its flamboyant pink, purple, and black paint job.

I dejectedly began the short drive home with my mouth turned down into a seemingly permanent frown as I contemplated the ruined summer that stretched ahead. My love life was an empty desert with no sign of life. I would most likely die at age ninety-eight a withered spinster, never having enjoyed the fruits of a love affair, let alone marriage. Then suddenly, as Wilma and I sat at an irritatingly long red light, my attention was drawn to my rearview mirror. Could it be? Yes!!! It's Bob! The light turned green and I watched anxiously to see if he knew it was me. Oh yes, dear readers, he follows me home, pulls up in front of my parent's cookie-cutter house in a post-World War II neighborhood, honks his horn, waves, and drives away with a gigantic grin on his adorably sweet face. Really? Hmm. Did this mean he *could* play a role in my seemingly ruined summer?

I didn't have much time to wonder, because that very same weekend I was off to San Diego with my sisters, Linda (the hazel-eyed brunette everyone referred to as the "smart one" for her la-de-dah 4.0 GPA) and Wilma (the blue-eyed ash-blonde known as the "cute one" for her sweet little button nose and tiny stature). This was our first ever, sisters-only, no parents allowed, carefully planned road trip. Upon arriving at the Vagabond Travelers Motel, we were shocked that the seemingly exorbitant price of $10.95 *per night* did *not* include breakfast, so we drank hot chocolate and ate peanuts from a vending machine in the morning. Saturday was spent being unabashedly touristy at Sea World, marveling at the treasures of the ocean—neon fish and bright coral and cute dolphins—and topping off the day by squealing mightily when Shamu the Killer Whale jumped his entire his body out of the water to snatch a fish from his trainer and sent a gigantic wave of water into our front row seats, totally soaking us when he splashed back down. That explained why no one else was sitting in our section. But the experience they missed was totally awesome! The surprise of the water drenching our bodies created a never to be forgotten, exquisite memory. I wish we had a picture of ourselves. Today there would be, on cell phones, on Facebook, on the news at five. But none back then.

The next morning, we checked out and happily headed home, only to soon realize we're lost when we don't remember there being any farms or ranches or dirt roads on our drive *to* San Diego. Surely it couldn't have changed *that* much in just one day? We asked for directions from a local ranch hand who was wearing a tattered straw hat, flannel shirt, and jeans. Stifling a laugh at our complete naivety, he pointed out we'd made a wrong turn in Oceanside but if we followed the road we were on and made a left at the next city, Corona, we'd be home in nothing flat. We thanked him profusely and blew him kisses as we drove away, and followed his directions carefully. Although arriving a couple hours later than anticipated, we pulled up in front of our pale yellow, white-trimmed house and, to our total surprise, it wasn't Mama's mint green and white 1957

Chevy Impala in the driveway. It was my Pimpmobile, freshly washed, waxed, and beautifully detailed! Perhaps it was Daddy's surprise graduation gift? I knew he liked me best!

I breathlessly rushed inside to find my parents enjoying an afternoon cup of coffee at the kitchen table. "Who washed my car?" I asked. After glancing at one another knowingly, my mom proudly announced that Bob—the boy from school, the new one in my class, the one who had followed me home—had come by to see me early Saturday morning. When told I was off on a weekend girls' trip, his face fell but he quickly recovered and asked, "Do you think she'd mind if I washed and waxed her car?" After winning their whole-hearted approval, he energetically spent all day Saturday working on my car and visiting with my parents and... And what? There's more? Mama had invited him over for Sunday dinner—oh my, that's tonight! Be still my little heart, the impossible had happened. My long, lonely summer was looking more like a hot and heavy romance by the second.

Needless to say, Bob and I began dating, and within a month he shockingly asked me to marry him and I petulantly told him, "Nonsense, you don't even know me, you silly boy! Talk to me in a year!"

Things went along innocently for the next few months, and then I turned eighteen. With no more threats of statutory rape, we began going further and further, until one night he begged me to let him "put just the tip in." I did. It felt unbelievable. So, the next time, he put the whole thing in, and what a *fabulous* feeling it was! How could society have

41

kept this heart-pounding, magical, blissful thing from us all our teenage lives?

Then my period didn't come. And still didn't come. I told him I thought our magical act had somehow gotten me pregnant and our lives would forever be ruined! We screwed (pardon the pun) up the courage to tell our parents, and were forbidden to be alone (like it mattered now that I was pregnant!!!) until the wedding two weeks later in our pastor's backyard. I was tainted, spoiled goods, and not allowed to wear white or invite anyone other than the immediate family to the hastily arranged wedding of two teenagers who had broken the cardinal rule of maintaining chastity until marriage.

The sex was fun, the embarrassment was agonizing.

The shame was magnified even more because, now that we could *legally* have sex and excitedly approached our marital bed on our honeymoon night, we could not figure out *how* to have sex on a totally flat double bed. Our only two experiences had been, you got it, twisting our bodies into pretzels in the backseat of a car. Apparently, fertility and lovemaking are enhanced when coitus is conducted in the backseat of a tiny, uncomfortable Volkswagen Beetle. Don't worry, it didn't take long for us to get the hang of doing "it" on a bed, and a few months later, our beautiful baby boy was ushered into this world—nearly three weeks early, shattering our hopes no one would realize I was pregnant when we got married.

Lesson 5: Fertility apparently increases in the backseat of a Volkswagen.

Chapter 6. Carol—And John

When I was a toddler, my parents began attending a conservative Baptist church. I learned to love the tranquility of the tiny chapel with its colorful stained-glass windows, including my favorite of Christ agonizingly praying to God the Father in the Garden of Gethsemane. Why this scene was so intriguing to me became apparent years later when I met my future nemesis.

I had always been the prettiest and smartest girl at my church, until the dark day when pretty and popular Carol showed up. My body had, by then, filled out into *va-va-voom* curves for my average height and I worked hard to tame my naturally curly, dirty dishwater blonde hair. Overall, not bad for a fourteen-year-old but much less classy than that darned Carol. Carol was a tall girl with long, thick, lustrous black hair, a classically beautiful face, and ever so elegant, especially when compared to my tomboyish demeanor. Many a prayer on bended knee (mimicking my favorite stained-glass picture) was sent to God by me begging Him to send this girl and her family to another church. Preferably far away.

Equally attractive and with excellent grades in school *and* a volunteer in the church's nursery, she—oh yes, *she*—just had to show me up by playing the *piano*. Growing up poor, my family could not afford piano or any kind of lessons. So, I joined the choir. Ha! She couldn't sing *and* play the piano at the same time, could she? So there, Carol with your long piano-playing fingers. The field was once again level. The rivalry continued as we tried to outdo each other with carefully coiffed hair, beautifully applied makeup, and cleverly chosen outfits complemented by stylish shoes.

Within a year of our graduation from high school, we were both engaged and married, she to John and me to Bob. Our first children's joyful births occurred just a few weeks apart. One Sunday morning, she and I arrived at the church nursery at exactly the same time. She with her (begrudgingly, I must admit) beautiful baby girl, Carol Ann, and me with my adorable infant son, Robbie. We looked at each other with disdain, then looked down to see our babies were fascinated with each other, softly cooing and blowing spit bubbles. At first, we turned beet red with embarrassment at our own childish behavior, compared to our children's innocent instant acceptance of one another. Then our faces softened and, in a microsecond, our silly rivalry was gone, replaced by a beautiful friendship that lasted the rest of her life.

Each of us had married a man who felt strongly that the man was the head of the household, going to work each day to support the family. In their minds, womenfolk belonged in the background taking care of the children, cooking, cleaning, and doing laundry, so our lives were nearly identical. A few years passed, during which Carol had two more little girls, Christy and Cindy, and I another little boy, Eddy. With more mouths to feed, both of our budgets needed a little supplementing so Carol gave piano lessons and I sold house wares at home parties. In spite of our hectic schedules, we spoke often on the phone, saw each other at church every Sunday, and every few weeks Carol and John and Bob and I double dated, leaving the children with their respective grandparents.

Life seemed perfect until one day Carol called to tell me she hadn't quite felt herself for a while. A low-grade fever and a dull, persistent ache in her chest just wouldn't go away, no matter what she tried. So, I watched her little girls while she went to the doctor, where she was diagnosed with an unknown infection. A few days later, test results confirmed she indeed was suffering from an infection, *inside her heart.* I'd never heard of such a thing, but antibiotics took care of the problem and she was okay...for a while. Two months later, she was back in the doctor's office. A lung infection was followed a few weeks later by a kidney infection.

As Carol's condition worsened, a panel of doctors, experts in various fields, convened. The specialists bombarded her with questions for hours and ultimately diagnosed her with a disease called lupus. Time after time, this beautiful thirty-two-year-old woman was hospitalized with a myriad of symptoms and infections. Then the migraine headaches began, with the excruciating pain keeping her bedridden for days.

Her husband was offered a great job opportunity, so in the midst of her treatment, they moved to Northern California. I missed her desperately. Phone conversations continued and I flew up often. The last time I saw Carol, she was hospitalized in San Francisco once again, taken by ambulance from their small town of Grass Valley. As soon as I got the news, I caught the next plane out of LAX to be at her side. It broke my heart to see her frail body hooked up to so many tubes and machines. Her beautiful face seemed to be sinking into her cheeks, her lovely body now skin and bones. I did my best to raise her spirits by giving her the latest news about family and church members, laughing until my sides ached when she begged me to tell the story about our rivalry as teenagers. Her wan smile was my reward, and I'll never forget the brief joy I brought her in spite of the pain and medications that left her barely conscious. Make a person laugh and they'll love you forever—right?

The time went so quickly and suddenly it was time to return to my own family. We said our tearful goodbyes and, after losing ourselves in hugs and kisses, I headed for the airport. Salty tears mixed with mascara trailed down my face as I stared sullenly out the taxi's window. A short time later, my body was on an airplane miles above the ground but my heart, oh my heart, stayed with my sweet friend.

Once home, normal activities were somehow resumed but thoughts and prayers for her constantly occupied my mind. A few days later, I came home to a message on my answering machine. It was from Carol. Still hospitalized, she asked me to call her as soon as I got home. It was late, after ten in the evening and I was so, so tired, so I blew her voice a kiss and whispered a promise to call in the morning after we'd both had a good night's sleep.

The following morning the sky was dark and gray. An ugly drizzle of dirty Los Angeles rain had turned sparkling, weekend-washed cars into dirty, spotted hunks of metal. As

I gazed out the window wondering if the rain would stop before I drove my sons to school, the phone rang. Oh no, it's Carol! I should have called as soon as I woke up.

I anxiously pick up the phone, immediately starting to apologize to Carol for not having called sooner. It wasn't her. It was her husband. John was sobbing into the phone that she was gone. "Gone where? Did she leave the hospital?" I asked. "No, she's dead, Diana. Her heart stopped sometime during the night, and the monitors failed to shriek their alarms."

No one knew she had stopped breathing for at least twenty minutes, which was when her nurse found her unresponsive and screamed for a crash cart. Carol's weak heart was shocked over and over until it began to beat faintly. The staff was elated until tests confirmed the worst. They had taken too long to revive her. There was no sign of life in her brain. Carol was brain dead.

John begged the doctors to keep her on life support, and held nightly prayer vigils over her body, but to no avail. A week later her body began to deteriorate and the distraught husband was forced to make the horrendously difficult decision to take his wife off life support. Her struggle was over. We lost that beautiful, gracious woman to an undetected brain aneurism that had grown to the size of a grapefruit before bursting. When John called again with that devastating news, I told him I'd call our friends, and Bob and I would be there as soon as we could make flight arrangements.

As I numbly replaced the phone in its cradle, my mind's eye literally saw her spirit being carried on angels' wings, her feet gently touching down at Heaven's Gate. St. Peter taking her hand and leading her to a path of gold that led to a pearl-white Steinway piano where she was placed gently on a white velvet stool. Instantaneously she began playing a celestial song of praise to her God, while a choir of celestial beings sang *"Glory, glory, glory."* I knew my Carol, my best friend forever, was at last out of pain and in a far better place. But our pain had just begun.

Those of us left behind gathered at her and John's home for one last weekend before the funeral. All of us were in our thirties, good friends since high school. We left our children at home with family, and Carol and John's girls— eleven, nine, and five years old—were at their grandparents' home. We were free to fully mourn our young friend without being burdened with the need to be brave for anyone. It was like something out of a movie with the seven of us, four couples minus our precious Carol, crying and hugging, consoling John first and then one another.

As the day wore on, our thoughts lightened and we talked and laughed like old times. Until one of us would stop laughing and suddenly look up, fully expecting to see Carol walk in the room. The realization that she was gone forever washed over us again and again throughout that weekend. The loss felt like scalding acid hitting us, jolting us into accepting she would *never* again join us, at least not on this earthly plane. And the hot tears coursed down our cheeks…again and again. It was almost too much for our minds to grasp, that never again could we talk to her, laugh with her, hold her, or hear her play the piano. She was totally and irrevocably *gone*.

The funeral was and still is a blur. After hugging the grieving husband, assuring John we were only a phone call away if he needed to talk and that we would always be there for him, we solemnly flew back to SoCal. Once home, I drew my family around me and held them close. At this being-an-adult-thing-is-no-fun age of thirty-two, I had been forced into accepting my own mortality. That life is extraordinarily fragile and can end in literally the blink of an eye. No one is guaranteed another day, let alone another breath.

Until then I had thought I would live forever—or at least until I was so wrinkled and saggy and slow and didn't care if I drew another breath. I pictured myself in a rest home swaying to Eric Clapton's version of "Knock Knock Knockin' on Heaven's Door" when death would come knockin' at my door. Maybe they should put it on my tombstone.

Here lies Diana Patricia O'Donnell
Born 1948—Died 2122
Still rockin' out when she kicked the bucket at 174

No one should die when they're young and vital. No one. No one. *No one.* It's simply not fair! My eyes burned; my chest ached. My mind screamed, *Let me wear sack cloth and ashes and a black arm band signifying to the world that I am in mourning, do not bother me!* For at least a decade, maybe two.

After a few weeks, my heartache had begun to subside but John's pain increased until he could stand it no longer. The two a.m. phone calls began. Always beginning with "I'm sorry to bother you but you said I could call any time. I was such an inconsiderate ass to Carol"—which he was—

"and should've helped her more. I didn't know she was in so much pain. I wish I hadn't yelled at her for not having the house clean when I got home from work. For scolding her for not having dinner ready and complaining about the laundry piling up. I wish I had known she was going to die but I didn't know. I didn't know."

Night after night. The same thing.

Each night, I sleepily assured him that Carol loved him more than anything. Agreeing with him that yes, he should have been a better husband but maybe it was a lesson he needed to learn. That we all needed to learn. Life's rollercoaster can derail into a pile of regrets anytime, anywhere. Today, tomorrow, or fifty years from now. So, live each day as though it were your last.

What else could I say? I wanted to slap him and tell him to quit whining. To grow up and be the father his kids needed. Instead, I urged him to mourn totally, completely, for one year, then move forward and let the regrets of the past go.

After a few months, the agonizing calls slowed to once a week, and then that first year passed. John called to ask if I thought he should attend a Christian three-day camp for single parents. I did, and assured him that Carol would certainly approve. She didn't want him to spend his life alone. For the girls to be deprived of a kind woman in their lives. So, he decided to go, entrusting Carol's parents with the care of his daughters, and left with hope in his heart. He was both cheered and saddened by the sheer number of single Christian parents who were there. Then, across the room he saw a woman. Unlike tall, dark haired Carol, Melanie was petite and blonde, with a soft laugh that sounded like bells tinkling. Small talk on a wooden bench near the chapel turned to admiration as each revealed their recent heartaches. She was a widow with three little girls the same age as his. Surely, she was a gift from heaven, John thought to himself as he bowed his head in silent thanks to God for this miracle.

After the camp ended, John and Melanie kept in touch by phone and soon they were dating. Despite the heartache of having lost their spouses quite recently, they fell into an easy and gentle love with one other. When the children finally met, the girls took to each other as if they had known each other forever. Before long, John began thinking of marriage. After discussing the possibility with his daughters, he secretly spoke to Melanie's daughters. To his delight, both sets of girls were beyond excited at the possibility of blending their two families into one. A few weeks later, John got down on one knee in front of all six girls and asked Melanie to do him the honor of marrying him and his girls. Through tears of joy she said yes, followed by all six girls squealing their approval and piling on top of the couple.

John nervously begged the same six of us who had gathered at his home for Carol's funeral to bestow our blessing on the holy union by attending the wedding. After much gnashing of teeth, gallons of shed tears, and "How could he do this so *soons*," we all agreed to attend the wedding in the lovely seaside city of Santa Barbara. With a gentle summer breeze caressing our cheeks and fluffy white clouds floating lazily in the bluer-than-blue sky, we arrived to give our reluctant approval. Solemnly we filed into the tiny church and with handkerchiefs in hand sat on the groom's side, waiting for the much-dreaded ceremony to begin.

Music floated gently to the ceiling as the organist's hands skimmed lightly over the keys. The minister, clad in black suit and white collar, stepped to the front of the church and was joined by John at his side. The music quickened with the opening chords of "Here Comes the Bride" and we rose from our seats along with the congregation. Collectively we held our breath and braced ourselves for the sight of another woman walking toward *Carol's* husband. Looking back to watch for "the Other Woman," instead of seeing the bride, we saw the six little girls standing shyly at the back of the church, lovely in matching pale pink lace dresses, with delicate white flowers adorning their beautiful long hair. Each held delicately woven reed baskets filled with tiny pink rose petals.

The organist smiled and switched to "Somewhere Over the Rainbow" as two-by-two, starting with the youngest, the girls—one his and one hers—walked down the aisle strewing petals as they made their way to the altar. Next came the middle two and finally the eldest, just thirteen years young, walking behind the bride. Our eyes, glistening with as yet unshed tears, grew wide with surprise. Turning to each other to confirm we were indeed seeing what our eyes seemed to be seeing, our mouths fell open and unrestrained tears poured down our faces. It was not the daughter. It was our beloved Carol walking toward us, holding the bride's veil along with her soon-to-be-sister. As they reached the front of the church and turned to face us, Carol's face vanished and her daughter, Carol Ann, stood before us.

Without a doubt, we knew it was Carol who appeared in her daughter's body, silently imploring the approval of the unification of two broken families into one whole, loving unit. None of us will ever forget that moment, when our friend left her heavenly home for a few brief moments to bless her husband's union.

Lesson 6: Live as though it could all end tomorrow. Never stop living. And never stop loving.

Chapter 7. Don't Let George Do It

The first few years of my marriage, I was busy with the birth and mothering of two young sons. Weekdays for Bob were filled with his job, and weekends were spent outside with yard chores or woodworking in the garage. Weekdays and weekends were monotonously the same for me—cooking, cleaning, bathing, and nourishing the kids' minds and bodies. Daily footage of the Vietnam War bombarded the television, reminding us of the constant chaos in the world. Somewhere along the way, we stopped being Bob and Diana, the loving couple, and became Mom and Dad, good parents but not-so-much-in-love couple. After seven years of marriage, our personal life was nearly non-existent except for occasional sex of the boring, non-fulfilling-to-me type followed by his gruff, "I love you. Good-night." One day, I'd had enough of being ignored by my own husband and asked for a divorce.

We were attending one of Bob's twice-yearly business conventions in one of the most romantic cities on this earth—Nice, France—when I had an epiphany. It happened unexpectedly. Both of us were dressed impeccably, my hair coiffed and makeup carefully applied. An uneventful evening of cocktails and dinner with Bob's associates had ended and, as we entered the hotel's elevator, my mind was quietly reliving the evening. It hit me that neither of us had spoken even one word to each other the entire evening. We held polite conversations with the other couples at our table but had said *nothing*, *nada, zilch* to one another since the night before's, "I love you. Good-night."

At that moment I knew, to the depth of my soul, my husband would be content married to literally any woman on this earth. That is, as long as she accompanied him to events, cooked, cleaned, raised his children satisfactorily, and met his occasional sexual needs. My head jerked back as I realized I meant no more to him than his favorite baseball cap. All there was between us was that we were both comfortable, dependable, and fit snugly in all the right places.

The elevator door opened and we walked silently to our room. Once inside, I calmly changed out of my evening clothes and into street clothes, and began packing my suitcase. Clearly perplexed, my husband asked what I was doing. "I'm leaving you. I want a divorce." Bob was genuinely stunned and asked me what brought this on. I told him I felt like nothing more than an accessory to him. Calmly, coldly, I explained. "There is no love left in our marriage and I want out." Scalding tears of remorse fell on his cheeks. He promised to change. "I'll do anything to save our marriage. I got so caught up with being a good provider I forgot I needed to be a good husband." Hoping against hope that he meant it, I gave him a chance to prove what he said.

Ten more years pass and things hadn't changed. Oh sure, the first couple of months he gave me compliments, helped with chores around the house a few times, and even brought me flowers—once. But soon it was the same old same old. Ours had become another loveless, miserable marriage in the suburbs of Los Angeles. You see, it's impossible to repair a broken relationship without using the right tools, and he refused to go to counseling or attempt to change any of the behaviors I found so frustratingly unbearable. He insisted I was the one who needed fixing, not him. That I should be thrilled he brought home a paycheck. Enough to pay all our bills, right? So, what was wrong with *me* that I didn't appreciate him? Why did I feel so lonely inside a marriage?

It was like driving in circles on a one-way street until I finally stopped the car and took off on foot alone, determined to find happiness. Could I find happiness without the security and comfort of a long-time marriage? I felt like I'd been alone for years anyway so why keep trying? We occupied the same home, the same bed, but spent no time *together*. There were no date nights. He even refused to join the family to see a movie or go to dinner or for a stroll on the beach. Never complimented me on a new outfit or hairstyle. Didn't even notice when I lost fifty pounds and went down eight dress sizes. I had become invisible to him. But I wasn't invisible to the rest of the world.

A handsome, much younger man *did* notice and said all the things I longed to hear. Soon George and I were enjoying a torrid affair that proved to be the final nail in the coffin of a very dead marriage.

You see, love can only conquer all if *both people* work at it. With give and take by both parties.

My never-one-to-be-humble advice to men and women out there is to take the time and effort to notice the little things. Tell your spouse regularly how much you love him or her. Tell her she's beautiful or he's handsome. Have date nights *alone*, as a loving couple. Passionately and regularly make love, because if you don't, there are plenty of people lined up like customers outside an electronics store on Black Friday who will gladly take your place in your neglected spouse's heart, mind, and bed.

Lesson 7: Love conquers all, but only if it's traveling on a two-way street.

Chapter 8. In the Wink of an Eye

With our marriage definitely on the rocks, I asked Bob if we could try having an open marriage in the hopes he would remember how to treat a woman. He agreed and we both dated others, but for me it was heartbreaking to watch him come home from work, take a shower, get dressed up, and walk out that door headed for another woman's arms. When Bob told me he thought he was falling in love with another woman, a *twenty-year-old*, I filed for divorce, went home, and wept bitterly the entire day.

My life was over. No longer would our teenage sons have the security of a two-parent home. Robbie and Eddy would be leaving me every other weekend for visits with their dad and his young girlfriend and I would have to hear about this *child* their dad had fallen for. I had been a stay-at-home mom my children's entire lives, supplementing my husband's income with a part-time job as a home party manager, and now I was faced with the nearly overwhelming fact that soon I would be *supporting* my family on my meager earnings plus whatever spousal and child support the court awarded me. The reality of my situation was not only frightening. It was disturbing, disarming, and downright terrifying. And so, I cried. And cried. And cried. All day long.

So, there I am that day, sitting in a growing puddle of my own pitiful tears when I realize today's Monday! I look nervously at the clock, begging it not to be too late. Okay, I've got an hour before my presence is required at a weekly sales meeting eleven miles away. Not only would my bosses be there but so would my own sales team, the women who looked up to me as their leader and mentor. I am their Rock of Gibraltar, for crying out loud (no pun intended). I quickly look in the mirror, dry my tears, and begin mentally transforming myself from a sad, pathetic creature to some semblance of a professional sales manager. The guiding light of women I had personally recruited for my sales team deserved the best! After splashing cold water on my face, applying fresh makeup, and fluffing my hair into my best Farrah Fawcett look, I'm ready to get dressed. By the time I finish putting on pantyhose, white blouse, dark navy business suit, and matching high-heeled pumps, I know I'm ready to take on anything. A deep, cleansing breath declares to the world *"Mission accomplished!"* and I walk out the front door with briefcase in hand and head held high.

Once inside my white Ford station wagon—a company car that required meeting a minimum group sales quota to drive or I would be hoofing it to my in-home parties—the blues again descended around me like dark storm clouds on a winter's day. "Don't cry, it's gonna be okay," I say over and over, while taking deep breaths to stop the inevitable waterworks from ruining my mask of makeup. Just then I hear an engine's loud roar and glance in my rearview mirror. A sports car is racing up behind me. Now mind you,

I'm boxed in on the slow lane of the 405 freeway and there's absolutely nowhere for me to go to get out of this maniac's way, so I watch in my rearview mirror as he slows down slightly to maneuver around me. I look to my left and there he is. A movie-star-gorgeous, black-haired, blue-eyed earth-bound god of a man in a brand new, white Chevrolet Corvette. He slows his speed to the 55 mph I was carefully maintaining. He looks over, smiles the smile of an aftershave model in a daytime soap opera commercial, winks at me, blows me a kiss, then surges ahead and is gone. A smile spreads across my now-beaming face and I feel young, strong, and powerful. And I flat out *know* my life is going to be okay.

I searched the traffic ahead for any sign of him but he was nowhere to be seen. Who was this stranger? I don't have a clue but tend to believe he was an angel sent from above.

Lesson 8: A wink and a smile can change a life forever.

Chapter 9. Edifying Eddy

For me, one of the most difficult transitions from married to divorced status was being a single parent. Bob had been the enforcer, me the consoler. Being the one the boys turned to for comfort when their father punished them was a role I truly relished. I loved holding them in my arms and telling them the world would not end because they were about to suffer through two *weeks* of no television or having to come straight home from school for a week, or no dessert for a month. As a single parent, *I* now was responsible for making the rules *and* doling out the punishment, at least when they were in my home. Was I up to it? We would soon find out.

On a night like any other soon after I filed for divorce, I was curled up on the sofa in my pajamas taking a much needed break from paperwork and housework when my youngest boy, Eddy, dressed in a clean t-shirt, jeans, and Nikes, his blonde hair neatly combed, walked past me toward the front door. He had been given his dad's old Honda Civic when he turned sixteen and was apparently feeling pretty sure of himself. Oh yeah, to him the punisher was out of the picture and he had free rein to do what he wanted.

One of the house rules had always included a ten-p.m. curfew on school nights. Since it was ten minutes to ten and this *was* a school night, there was no possible way he could go anywhere and get back in time for curfew. I had no choice but to confront him. "Where do you think you're going? This is a school night."

My six-foot tall man-child looked down at me, his five-foot-five mom, scowled, and retorted, "Out." Then, looking directly in my eyes, he said, "What are you going to do about it?"

I knew this was a pivotal moment in our relationship and what I said next would either solidify my image as a strong parent or his mind would morph me into a puppet, willing to do anything to keep the peace.

Silently, I walked around him, blocking the front door. "Eddy, if you walk out this door tonight, you will never walk through it again. So, think carefully before you take your next step."

I didn't realize how tall he had grown until that very second. I felt tiny as I stared up into his face.

The challenge stunned him into silence as he tried to determine if I meant what I said, before finally muttering, gruffly, "Fine, I'll stay in." He turned to go back to his room.

"Oh no, we're not finished," I said, knowing we had to come to an understanding about who was in charge. "You have three choices. First choice, go live with your father. Second choice, live under my roof with my rules. Third choice, I can turn you over to the State and forget I ever had you." I could feel my blood pressure rising, adrenaline flowing. Now I was literally shaking in my boots (well, really my house slippers). Terrified of the choice he might make but too late to back down now, I had to go through with my bluff.

Flashes of him as the colicky baby I'd rocked the first three months of his life, the child whose tears I'd wiped from his face when he skinned his knee. The young man I would literally lay down my life for was now challenging my authority. My resolve began to falter. Looking up at his face, I almost crumbled but saw a hint of fear in his eyes and panic beginning to rise in his chest. His cheeks turned blood red. He opened his mouth to speak and I threw the final blow.

"Eddy, you have twenty-four hours to make your decision." I dramatically glanced at the sunburst clock on the wall to verify the time. "Ten o'clock tomorrow night, we meet here to further discuss your options. Be prepared to give me your decision. Now go to bed. I'll see you tomorrow night."

Early the next morning, I was in the kitchen making breakfast when an obviously very anxious Eddy walked in. My hands were shaking so hard I had to hide them in the pockets of my apron.

"Mom, I don't want to wait until tonight. Let's talk about this before I go to school," he begged.

Without turning from the stove, I calmly replied, "I said ten tonight and that's when we'll talk. Think long and hard about your decision. It will change your life forever."

That afternoon, in walked my son from school, head hung low, tears brimming in his pale blue eyes while he pleaded, "Mom, please. I don't want to wait until tonight. Please, please, please can we talk about it now?"

I motioned for him to sit at the dining room table. "Okay, let's talk. Shall we go over your options or have you already made your decision?" I said, ashamed I'd let it escalate this far.

Words spilled out of his mouth like a tidal wave. "I don't want to live with Dad. He's even stricter than you and I can't stand his new girlfriend. She's barely older than me and tries to boss me around all the time." A huge wave of relief washed over me. Tears streaming down his face, he continued. "And I don't want you to give me over to the State and forget you ever had me! I love you, Mom, and I am so sorry for being such a total jerk last night. I love you so much and want to stay here and live under your roof, by your rules."

He's my baby boy again. Tears stream down my face and I am so, so grateful he chose to stay with me. We hug each other for a long time, pull apart, and I ask him to sit down again. We need to make his decision official. I walk across the room, retrieve a pen and notebook from a drawer in my desk, and return to the dining room table.

"House rules and punishments," I said as I opened the notebook and put pen to paper beginning with the sentence, *On this day my son, Edward Patrick O'Donnell, has agreed to live under my, his mother's, Diana Patricia O'Donnell, roof until said son graduates from high school or turns 18 years old, whichever comes first, and agrees to abide by the following rules and punishments to be enforced by me, his mother.*

Next come the rules. We agree on each one, including curfews on school nights and non-school nights. Coming straight home from school unless prior permission had been granted. Required household chores, and so on.

After the rules were established, I declared that the punishments were to be set by him—and him alone. Without hesitation, Eddy set the consequences for breaking each rule. Although his punishments were harsher than I would have inflicted, we agreed he knew himself best. We signed and dated the House Rules and, with the paper in hand, I left to make copies at Thrifty's, the local drug store.

For the next eighteen months, the house rules were retrieved whenever Eddy broke one, which wasn't often, and punishment was doled out accordingly. On his eighteenth birthday, we stood side by side as he burned the rules in the backyard hibachi, and then hugged. To this day, we have a wonderfully close relationship. By working together to find a solution we had gained respect for one other, and have since worked together many times, always as equals.

What would've happened if I had let him walk out the door that night? We'll never know but I have a feeling it may have ended badly for both of us. Him being convinced he could do anything without consequences. Me knowing I had failed at being the kind of strong mother he needed.

Lesson 9: Being a single parent has its drawbacks, but also has its rewards.

Chapter 10. Willie Is (Almost) Always Wonderful

Even though I felt stronger both professionally and as a single parent, at thirty-five years old, five-foot five-inches, and 135 pounds, I felt old, fat, and ugly. My ego had been shattered like a cheap mirror and needed a good bit of superglue to put it back together. (Eventually I came to the conclusion that *perhaps* a man could get past me being *old, fat,* and *ugly* but what about—gasp! —my *stretch marks*?) Friends suggested I try nightclubbing. They were right. The wild discos of the eighties allayed all my fears. Lots of men asked me to dance and, at the end of every evening, shy ones asked for my phone number while bold ones did their best to convince me to go home with them for a "drink," wink wink.

I was astounded by the attention. What could they possibly be thinking? Can't they see my body is beginning to sag? Boobs are starting to droop. A flock of crows' feet having taken up permanent residence around my eyes. Wayward hairs beginning to grow on my chin. The pale blonde mustache over my lip makes me look like a pre-pubescent boy or an ancient man, I'm not sure which. Then there's the horrible, the dreaded, the impossible-to-ever-completely-get-rid-of—drum roll please—*stretch marks* covering my breasts, stomach, and butt like a road map of the United States of America. Quite shockingly, I discovered that *none* of it matters because I have that precious prize between my legs I playfully named Precocious Patty. And precocious she was (and still is), with a mind of her own.

Discovering a man's "little head" rules the "big head" made me feel a little like Columbus discovering America and soon my own journey of discovery began. I finally got it that I was not old, fat, *or* ugly, and men apparently don't mind stretch marks because not one man has ever said even one word about them. With all the machismo most men wear like Fonzie's leather jacket, they are far more insecure than we women. The male population is absolutely, totally, obsessed with being assured that their lovemaking is not only adequate, every one of them is hoping, yes praying to every god they've ever heard of, that he's the *best* the lady has ever had. To tell the truth, I don't see that much difference unless the man's totally HUGE or really TINY, but guys care. Deeply. While bathing in the afterglow of that first lovemaking session, most men hold you tenderly then, without looking in your eyes ask if you enjoyed it. When the woman says yes, the real questions follow. Are you sure it was big enough? Good enough? Long enough. Wide enough. Hard enough. And so on. (Now guys, if you got your woman off does any of it really matter?) They all, and I mean every bleeping man, need reassurance that their masculinity was more than sufficient in the moment.

Something really odd to me is that so many below-average sized guys brag about their manhood before the clothes come off and then expect me to be impressed (like I

67

can't see what's right in front of my face) when their shorts are dropped. The dilemma is, to be truthful or not? What I really want to say is, "Honey, you're fooling yourself if you think there is anything special about that little thing of yours." Personally, I can't bring myself to say that to any man so I generally choose to bolster their obviously fragile egos by generically exclaiming, "Oh wow, I am impressed." All the while I'm secretly wondering if they have ever taken the slightest peek at the other guys in a public restroom. Wouldn't they have noticed they are way smaller? (Individual research queries have proven to me that men *do not* look at each other's privates at public urinals or gym showers. To look or judge or compare is flat-out forbidden. At least that explains the inability to accurately judge the size of their own Johnsons.)

Let's examine this phenomenon a little further. The guys with the really tiny ones are almost always embarrassingly apologetic before the clothes come off. This to me is sad. Small ones are actually much easier to satisfy orally or internally and generally it's over so quickly you barely break a sweat. These guys are just thrilled anyone wants to fool around with them, so it doesn't take much to make their day. Hooray for the guys with the little ones!

Inconsiderate men with not-so-big ones shove it in as soon as the woman starts to get turned on but hasn't had a chance to get a good look at his stuff. Like he's hoping we won't notice the size, and then tries to make up for being on the short side by proclaiming "women's nerve endings only go an inch or so into the vagina."

"Who are they kidding?" shouts Precocious Patty. "My nerve endings go all the way to my cervix, buddy. So, knock off the bullshit." Pardon her vulgarity, but you gotta consider where she lives. Down there, between my legs.

Truly considerate, pretty much average sized guys work hard to make up for their perceived short-comings (pun intended) by romancing a woman's entire body. These wonderful men stimulate all five (and sometimes six) senses orally and/or manually before the final plunge. The best of these lovers expand foreplay into a near Olympic event, while others master the art of postponing ejaculation by retreating, going back to foreplay for extended periods of time, then re-entering, again and again, until he is certain the woman is fully satisfied, evidenced by her limp body and low whimpering. Then and only then does he allow himself to climax.

Then there are the guys with the larger than average Jimmy Johns. They're the ones who love to show off their length to the woman. Drop their drawers and wait for the gasps. "Do you think you can handle it?" they slyly ask. Patty's like, "Heck yeah, I can handle you. Get that thing over here." But then a little foreplay, spit on the palm and wham, bam thank you ma'am, it's over way too quick for my taste. I like to take my time and enjoy every minute. So I'll take an average or smaller than average sized guy who takes pleasure in making a woman so happy she screams, over a big guy out to please himself first.

There's one size left to explore. The poor guys with the really huge ones. They suffer. Yes, I said suffer. Take the case of Aldus. Six-foot, nine-inches tall, the man said he couldn't play basketball to save his soul. Precocious Patty and I met him at a nightclub and, after quite a few drinks, we just had to ask him if everything was as big as he was.

"You're more than welcome to find out for yourself at my place."

Alrighty-dighty, the big guy had thrown down the gauntlet and I just had to know for myself. And we did. Aldus literally had a foot-long Dodger dog.

When he unveiled his manhood, Patty wanted to run screaming across the room wailing, "No way. Uh-uh. Never. You ain't getting near me with that pogo stick!" I told her to shut up and, after promising not to let her get hurt, we tried our best to accommodate him missionary style. Way too painful. So, Patty and I took over and climbed on top, going ever so slowly. Nope. He hit the end of the track long before the train had pulled all the way into the station.

To other men it would seem a dream come true but, sadly he, at thirty-six years old, had yet to find a woman who could take all of him. He had to be very careful not to injure a woman's insides with that gigantic member of his, so wild thrusting and bucking was definitely out. Despite his disappointment, Aldus thanked me for trying and said perhaps we could try again another time. Patty put her foot down and made me promise never, never, never again. Would he ever find total satisfaction? I hope so. Maybe a seven-foot-tall Amazon woman could handle him?

Lesson 10: Yes, size matters. To the man.

Chapter 11. Juan and Two

It's the eighties and nightclubs have popped up everywhere. "Nothing but meat markets," the oldsters claimed, because most of us who frequented them were looking for one thing. Well, three. Drinking, dancing, and a good roll in the hay. So off I headed to the nightclubs. Night after night. One glorious evening, I was having a fabulous time at a club in Lomita, California and in walked a tall, dark, and handsome Latino. He spotted me across the room. I saw him watch me toss back a shot of whiskey and follow that by a long pull on an ice-cold bottle of Coors. What a sight this man was, shiny black hair slicked back from his forehead. Skin, the color of hot desert sand. Red satin shirt unbuttoned halfway to his navel, revealing a muscular, hairless chest. Black leather pants tighter than the skin on a panther. High-heeled boots shined to a glossy sheen. I'm talking 1980s eye candy to the max.

He threaded his way through the crowded bar and was soon by my side with two shots, a saltshaker, and lime wedges. After placing the small tray on the bar, he turned, raised one eyebrow, indicated the empty seat next to me and asked, "May I join you?" I gestured my consent with a swish of my meticulously manicured hand. After he positioned his tight, perfect butt on the bar stool, he smiled and said, "My name is Juan the Great. What's your name, senorita?" I shrugged while giving him a sideways glance and a half smile. "Well, Juan the Great, my name is Diana, Dancing Goddess of the Disco."

Precocious Patty, who had been lounging in a temporary coma until Juan sat down, perked up, whistling. I immediately agreed with my little friend and the artful dance of flirtation began. Patty, the naughty, petulant creature that lives between my legs, was feeling quite randy earlier that evening when she insisted on helping me dress. Dark blonde hair piled high on my head. Heavy makeup that accentuated my sapphire blue eyes. Pale pink lipstick shimmering on rose petal-soft lips. Midnight blue spaghetti-strap dress that hugged my voluptuous body. Black snakeskin spike heels to finish the look. Precocious Patty and I were ready for love in all the right places.

Looking and sounding like a young Antonio Banderas, Juan teased, "May I show you the Latino way to drink your next shot?"

"By all means," I replied with a slightly bored expression. Juan continued, "These are shots of *tequila* but you must use the right technique to fully enjoy the experience." Taking my right hand, palm down, he licked the area between my index finger and thumb (which caused Patty to perk up even more), shook salt onto the wetness, and did the same to his own hand. He then leaned down, licked the salt off my hand, drank the shot in one gulp, slammed the glass down on the bar, and immediately sucked on a lime wedge. After waiting a moment for dramatic effect, his eyes like hot embers and a slight smile playing on his lips, he whispered in my ear, "Now it's your turn." This guy is frigging *hot*! My heart and mind are racing. Patty's starting to pant. Lick, drink, suck. Okay got it. Not complicated at all.

With shot glass raised I purred, "To new experiences." Never taking my eyes off his, I raised his hand to my lips. Licked the salt off his hand. Tossed down the shot. Then stick my tongue in the glass to seductively clean the last remaining drops. Slammed the shot glass on the bar, then sucked on the lime.

With his liquid brown eyes literally twinkling like stars on a clear winter's night, he said, "Oh, you are going to be a handful." He chuckled and raised two fingers to the bartender. Really, the peace sign? What's with this guy? I thought we had a real moment going on. Ooooh but *noooo*, here comes the bartender. Juan was ordering two more shots. Oh my, this night is going to be fun.

Talking led to laughing and dancing oh so closely until it was last call. My look must have been one of disbelief as the lights slowly came up and the bartender shouted out, "Last call," because Juan smiled, kissed me on the forehead, and asked, "Would you like to join me for a nightcap at a bar that never closes? Mi casita."

Casita? What the hell was that? He saw I was a bit perplexed and murmured, "My home, my little house. My car is parked just outside."

Patty had remained wide-awake since the moment Juan had appeared and was now begging me, "*Please*! He's pretty, he's really pretty, I want him. I want him *now*." I ignored her and told him I never went anywhere without my own car. Between his gentle pleading and Patty's frantic urging, I eventually agreed to follow him to his home in the hills of Palos Verdes for a drink and to watch the Johnny Carson show.

During the short drive, Patty kept up a running conversation with herself. Wondering how big the house was. What kind of nightcap he would serve. The size of his television. The size of his maleness, and if he knew how to use it to pleasure a woman. Will those full, beautiful lips of his kiss on my lips as well as Patty's. The size of his bedroom. If he had a waterbed. "I love waterbeds," Patty shouted, "I love them because long after the hip action stops, the bed keeps moving." Finally, I give Patty "the look" and shout at her to shut up or I'd put her chastity belt on, turn around, and go home. She shrugged and glared. "Well, it was *my* idea to come to his, how did he say it, yeah, 'casita.' So if he's as good as I think he is, you'll have me to thank," she pouted.

It was late and by the time we got to his casita, the *Tonight Show* had ended. Juan offered to show me around his home and I graciously accepted. The tour began in the sunken living room, complete with bullfighter paintings on the wall and a hand-carved mesquite wood dry bar where he poured Presidente brandy in short, round crystal snifters. Double doors from the living room revealed a large, meticulously landscaped backyard overlooking the Pacific Ocean. With his arm around my shoulder, we listened to the soothing sound of the waves as they kissed the waiting sand and I turned slightly, leaning into him for that first and oh-so-wonderful meeting of our lips. I was still swooning a bit when he took my hand and guided me to a side door that led to his bedroom. Patty took over from there. With that much tequila in our systems, followed by our snifters of brandy, the bedroom antics were intense but over way too soon. My Latin lover lay sprawled on the bed, snoring like a drunken burro, but I was still wide-awake.

As I stared through the window at the moon's reflection on the ocean, my stomach started growling like a hungry brown bear. I realized I'd forgotten to eat dinner, again. I wandered out of his room and eventually found my way to the kitchen. There, I was shocked to see an older version of tequila boy, Juan the Great. He was pouring himself a glass of milk and munching on a Mexican sweet bread.

"Well, hello there, beautiful. You must be the disco goddess my roommate—actually, he is my nephew—was determined to find tonight. My name is Antonio. What shall I call you?"

Well, ya gotta picture it, I'm in nothing but my Latin lover's undershirt, trying desperately to pull it down in the front and the back at the same time, my face and neck blushing as red as the lipstick on a Fifth Avenue hooker on a Saturday night. I finally managed to squeak out, "Hi. My name is Diana. I didn't know Juan and I weren't alone."

It turned out that Antonio was a professional chef at a five-star restaurant and had just arrived home. He insisted on whipping up cheese and green chili omelets with freshly made guacamole and warm, homemade flour tortillas. Just as I sunk my teeth into the first sumptuous bite, in walked bleary-eyed Juan, looking for me. Antonio praised his nephew on his good taste in women and asked, in front of me, if Juan would mind if he asked me out.

Juan looked at me, then announced quite clearly that he had no intention of sharing me that night or any night, for that matter, but I could decide on my own which, both, or neither I would like to date. After looking back and forth between the two, equally exquisite men, I gave both the permission to call me.

Dating roommates most certainly presented challenges, especially because I kept ending up in the wrong bed after late night trips to the bathroom. Eventually I stopped dating both Juan and Antonio. Looking back on it now, I kinda wonder if they sometimes switched beds on purpose just to mess with me. Who knows, it was the eighties and my goodness, did I have fun.

Lesson 11: Never date roommates at the same time.

Chapter 12. Kevin Got It When I Didn't

Kevin was a good friend of mine. Six feet tall, red headed, body hard and lean as a high school quarterback, with the chiseled face of a male runway model. We never dated. We were just good friends and could talk about anything. And we did, often. One bright summer day, he invited me over for one of our philosophical afternoons. There we are, me in shorts and a tank top, him bare-chested in Hawaiian trunks. Kicking back in Adirondack chairs, eating pretzels, and drinking beer like there's no tomorrow.

Down the street, we see a man and woman strolling along the sidewalk, hand in hand. He stops, takes a step back, looks in her eyes, and says something that makes her laugh. He pulls her in close and kisses her gently on each eyelid, then firmly on the lips. As they come closer, we can see them more clearly. He's tall, at least six-four, and handsomer than a hero on the cover of a romance novel. Curly brown hair, neatly trimmed mustache and goatee, lips as kissable as a newborn baby's cheeks. Wearing khaki cargo pants, tight lemon-yellow tank top, and brown sandals. Then there's the woman. Short, dumpy, and plain. Dressed in knit neon orange pants and a baggy white t-shirt with a big sunflower on the front. White socks and ugly black walking shoes complete her atrocious outfit. Mousy, straight, ash blonde hair. And the most beautiful laugh I've ever heard.

After they turn the corner, I shake my head. "Okay. Here's the first question of the day. Look at that couple that just walked by. Why would a good-looking man go for a plain Jane? All right, I'm gonna say it, downright ugly woman? *Why* on earth would someone like *him* want to be with *her*? Do the studly guys want to get all the attention, so they go for ugly girls or what?"

Kevin cocks his head to one side and looks at me like I'm nuts. "Are you kidding me? You really don't know the answer to that question? Let me see if I can explain it to you, seeing as how you're a *girl* and all."

I bristle at this insult, take a swig of my beer, burp loudly to prove I'm as much of a man as he is (actually even better because my species has a 'wo' in front of 'man,' so there), squint my eyes menacingly, and say, "You're cruisin' for a bruisin'. This better be good."

"You gotta understand I'm not badmouthing you ladies, but us guys can get any kind of woman we want. Fat ones, short ones, tall ones, skinny ones, smart ones, dumb ones, gorgeous or ugly. I done 'em all, so I know what I'm talking about. By the time a man is finished with all the young man shenanigans and is ready to finally settle down, he wants a woman he can talk to after he rolls off, you know? Someone to enjoy having an intelligent conversation with after sex is over, when he lights up a cigarette and finishes off the drink on the nightstand. His body's satisfied but his brain is yearning for a little stimulation. Maybe he'd like to discuss the current state of the union or where the stock market is headed. Or last night's Cubs game when the runner was obviously out at second but called safe. Or what needs to be done to eliminate the national debt. You know, important stuff like that.

"Like it or not, all women have the same physical attributes," he continues. "Legs that go from the floor to their hips. Arms that were made to wrap around a man's body. A mouth, two breasts, usually, and their own version of Precocious Patty. So why be with a woman just because she's pretty if there's nothing going on in the cerebral area? If the only thing she talks about is"—Kevin's voice rises three octaves— "what an absolutely horrid experience it was when I broke my nail trying to open a bottle of wine all by my*self*."

I got it.

So, ladies, keep up on current events, sports, business, and politics so you at least have an inkling of what's going on in the world. And remember to keep your lover stimulated outside the body, you know what I mean?

Keep in mind that engaging in conversation is fine and wonderful but you might not want to start an argument in bed if you're hoping to take up where you left off after you've both had a chance to recuperate.

My advice is to listen, interject here and there, and then—if you're like me and the first round was hopefully a preview of coming attractions—sneak back into the lovemaking. Or as Precocious Patty likes to say, "Ya gotta lead that horse back to the watering hole and make him think he's still thirsty."

Lesson 12: Sometimes a man wants to talk after he rolls off.

Chapter 13. Henry Kissinger Isn't for Kissing

Every woman's dream lover is one who is heart-stoppingly attractive, romantic as the day is long, a good conversationalist, and absolutely awesome in bed. Unfortunately, most men do *not* possess all four ideal qualities. Admit it, ladies, if he's a good lover we can forgive almost any shortages in the other three departments. Heck, I've felt lucky if he had even one.

For most of us, we will never meet a dream lover. Let's face it: by the time we reach our thirties, expectations tend to be downgraded by a lot. I mean *a lot*. They're attractive if they show up at your door freshly shaved with hair neatly combed, teeth brushed, and wearing a shirt that did *not* come off the bottom of the pile of clothes in the corner of the bedroom. A romantic evening usually involves tearing your clothes off *after* you get in the house instead of in the car, wham bam thank you ma'am. Then comes the lovemaking part.

So, let's get down to it. There are some men who are fantastic in bed but not much else. Great with his hands, mouth, and Willie, and would be an outstanding catch *if* he would just learn to keep his mouth shut—except, of course, when using it to pleasure his woman. These types of men are what I lovingly refer to as my "Come Hither Calls." A late-night call from me is an invitation to join me for a night filled with raucous behavior and little else. After the first roll in the hay, we women know if a man is a "keeper" or not. If we wish to keep him for wonderful nights on the town or dancing until dawn, or well, he's an excellent candidate for come-hithering, if you get my drift.

How does one get on my Come-Hither list? He's not good at socializing. He is self-centered enough to be flattered that he pleases me sufficiently to have earned a late-night call. The only thing that can really turn me off on these wild nights of personal satisfaction is if my invited guest insists on *talking* before plunging headfirst into a night of ecstasy. Telling the same boring stories over and over again. Constantly complaining about work or family or politics or sports. About buying stuff they could never afford in a zillion years.

We women open the door scantily clad, drink in hand, and ready for playtime expecting to be swept off our feet and carried into the bedroom. But no, the man walks through the door and wants to *talk*. Yep, opens his big mouth and out spills every disappointment the world has dealt him that week. We down our drink and patiently wait for the ranting to end so we can get on to the fun stuff, wishing just once we could say, "Look buddy, you are nothing more than a human dildo to me so just knock off all the chatter, okay? Sex is what I want. I like being with you because your body is warm and you don't take batteries. Period. If I wanted conversation, I'd be dating Henry Kissinger."

A couple examples from my own life may help you understand the concept, so here we go. There was this hotel casino executive I'll call Benny the Jet, who loved, loved, *loved* to hear himself talk. Constantly bragging about the rich and famous people he knew and how much his billionaire clients adored him. Naming every single hotel he'd managed around the world, the travel agencies he "used to own" (like, *who cares?*), the pathetic escapades of his limo driver/body guard. *Yawn*!!! All the while Benny the Jet's blathering on and on, I'm thinking to myself, "Hey, you are nothing but a glorified butler catering to all, and I mean all, these rich guys' wants and needs. Hookers willing to sleep overnight with a client in a coffin (eeeww!). Tickets to a sold-out boxing match. Fresh fish caught in the virgin waters of a yet-to-be-discovered lake halfway across the world. Agreed, you're The Man when it comes to all that. But you are *not* their friend. You're just a means to an end. If you were replaced tomorrow by a robot, it would not make a damn bit of difference to them, as long as they get what they want when they want it."

So, why did I put up with his one-sided conversation? Because he was really—and I do mean really, like *outstandingly* good—in the bedroom. But the boring chatter has got to go. He'd be the perfect dildo if his vocal cords were permanently removed. So that he could service me in *silence*. Oh wow, that sounds harsh but I'm truthing here, okay? A girl wants what she wants when she wants it without having to listen to all the boring bullshit.

Another guy—let's call him Motormouth Man-Candy—loved to talk about his dirt bike. His KTM something something that he literally lived to ride on the weekends. Yes, his bike was pretty cool, but how many times does a woman need to hear about it or the next bike he has his eye on? Or constantly whining about how mean his coworkers are to him. Oh boo-hoo! Or insisting, on his day off, we drive by the house he is aching to buy, when he's got such bad credit, he can't even buy a roll of toilet paper on credit. What's the sense in that?

I guess if you like kidding yourself, it's a good thing, but if you have a lick of sense it's like torturing yourself to ache for something you refuse to work toward. Okay, so you can see the man drove me nuts with his apple-pie-in-the-sky yearnings and complaining, but when it came to making me swoon in the horizontal or vertical, or really *any* position for that matter (he knew them all, I must say) and he got the highest A+ rating as Outstanding Human Dildo. This one can keep his vocal cords, I'll just learn to crank up the stereo and tune him out.

This lesson is for you guys out there so sit up and pay attention. If you notice your woman is gritting her teeth or dozing off while you're pillow-talking the same old boring crap we've heard again and again, you might consider resigning yourself to the obvious. Just keep your mouth shut and make Precocious Patty's sisters out there deliriously happy. Save those boring, repetitive stories and ridiculous, asinine opinions for your buddies at the bar, and use that mouth of yours for what it was created for. To make your woman scream in pleasure.

Lesson 13: Some men should be content with their role as a damned good human dildo.

83

Chapter 14. Right on the Mark. Sigh

Back in the nineties when the whole sexual harassment* mania began and I kept hearing about women in my company filing sexual harassment claims, I was feeling a bit left out. I could not think of a single incident where anyone had said anything inappropriate to me. I wanted in on the action. So, I tried wearing higher heels and shorter skirts. Nothing. More makeup and wilder hair. Nothing. Lower cut blouses and tighter belts. Nothing.

One day I went into my boss's office. Mark was a happily married man with a stay-at-home wife and four stair-step kids. I quietly closed the door and asked him, point blank, "Okay. Women are suing for sexual harassment all over the place and I have yet to be harassed, sexual or not, by anyone. I'm feeling left out." Mark looked up from his paperwork, took a deep breath, and tediously said, "Diana, you cannot harass the willing."

My face fell as I realized the truth. I was too willing. I had earned a bit of a reputation at my company, following an unintended Halloween costume malfunction, sort of, my first year in my job, and here it was still haunting me six years later.

Newly divorced, poor as a church mouse living with its mother on the bad side of town, I had learned the entire office was getting dressed up for Halloween. There were *prizes* to be won and everything. What? Halloween was one week away, and I didn't have any costumes and not one extra penny to buy anything even at a thrift store. But I had to go for it. So, I dug through my closets and drawers and finally found, thrown in the corner of the closet, a bright turquoise gauze beach cover-up that had been ruined by a splash of bleach on the front. A light bulb went off in my mind's eye. I soak the ruined dress in hot water and bleach, washed it, and hung it to dry. Voila! It came out white as the driven snow, perfect for the creepy-as-heck, undead creature I pictured I'd be.

Halloween arrived and I prepared for the day. My shoulder length brown hair was made scraggly with clear, caked hair gel. White face makeup and black "holes" for eyes made my face barely recognizable. More makeup helping to make the flesh on my arms appear to be ready to fall off. Bleached white dress thrown on. Uh-oh. My underwear could be seen through the thin gauze. Off came the white bra and panties and on went pale tan panties and tan bra. Nope, I can still see the bra, so off it goes. I looked in the mirror and realized, since the dress was so loose, no one could tell I wasn't wearing a bra—as long as the room wasn't too cold and the girls stayed warm, right? Of course it helped to have breasts still pretty perky for a thirty-eight-year-old woman. I looked doggone good as an undead creature. Off to work I went, wondering what prize I would win.

As the new girl at work, I didn't have any friends to critique my outfit before arriving at the office. Which, looking back now, would have maybe been a *really* good idea. All I knew was that I thought I looked pretty good compared to the Raggedy Anns, scarecrows, hobos, and other boringly average costumed co-workers I saw arriving for work. The morning went quickly and the noon judging was about to begin. We all lined up in the lunchroom, where the afternoon sun streamed through the windows. There were a few giggles and some finger pointing but I had no idea why. I didn't know they were looking at *me.* Much to my chagrin, I came in third place, and instead of the twenty-five-dollar cash prize I was handed a roll of 35mm film. I didn't even own a camera. Dejectedly, I returned to my desk.

The next day, my boss, Larry, who had been away on business the day before, called me into his office. "Diana," he said, "did you enjoy the office Halloween party yesterday?"

"Yes, I did, Larry. But I only won third prize and I thought I looked good enough to win first." A handful of pictures were spread across his desk. "Are there any pictures of me in the photos?" Gravely, Larry said, "Umm, yes there are. Now, Diana, I'm sure you were not aware of it, but when you stood in the lunchroom's sunlight yesterday it lit up your body like a neon sign. Human Resources instructed me to tell you to never, ever wear that costume to work again."

Even after all these years, I can still see the amused look on my boss's face and feel the shame and horror as I thumbed through picture after picture of me standing in the sun, nipples dark and erect, the shape of my voluptuous figure clearly outlined through the thin, gauze dress. I left his office, head down, sniffling just a little. The incident was quickly laid to rest by HR, my boss, and me, but the rest of the employees—even the ones not there that day but who heard about it through the office gossip mill—still remember the incident some thirty years later as if it were yesterday.

So, there it was. I had been outed as a wayward half-naked woman, too willing to accept a pass. From then on, fearful male co-workers steered clear of me. If anyone had made one, they knew I would have been grateful, flattered, maybe even reciprocated with a pass or two of my own.

Lesson 14: You can't sexually harass the willing.

*Major disclaimer here. I am well aware that sexual harassment is very real and must not be tolerated by anyone, male or female. I am just lucky to have never experienced it myself, so don't start sending letters, okay?

Chapter 15. Roger Wasn't Just Randy

This chapter has turned out to be by far the most difficult to write. To even force myself to recall the incidents is, to put it mildly, terrifying. It's true I admit to being a sexy, flirty, fun-loving woman but I guarantee I did not invite this. Even though these incidents happened many years ago, the memories have the raw and very real power to make my heart pound and palms sweat.

Okay, deep breath. Here we go.

The first was a seemingly innocent late-night breakfast date with a man I met just before a nightclub closed. Randy was obviously successful, dressed in a designer suit and tie, and had sprinted over to ask me to dance the last dance. After the music ended and the lights came up, he invited me to breakfast at a local coffee shop. As was my cardinal rule, I drove myself there. In the harsh glare of the café lighting, I saw he was fiftyish, with dark brown hair graying at the temples. He squinted a little so I assumed he was too vain to put on his glasses.

We ordered breakfast and enjoyed light conversation about the Dodgers. The mild weather we'd been enjoying in Southern California. Favorite music—his, hard rock seventies; mine, popular music, a little on the softer sixties side. Once we finished eating, he excused himself to use the restroom and was gone so long that I thought I'd been stuck with the bill. Just as I was preparing to pay and go home, he slid back in the booth, grabbed my hand, tossed a twenty-dollar bill on top of the tab, and rushed me outside, holding my hand so tightly it was beginning to hurt.

His actions were definitely more aggressive after returning from the restroom and I admit I heard faint alarm bells going off as I absently wondered if he had taken drugs in the men's room. Randy calmed down a little and thanked me for taking the time to have breakfast with him, and politely insisted on driving me to my car since it was parked several rows away and it was so late. Against my better judgment I agreed, and climbed into his white Mercedes Benz.

As he pulled near my car he stopped, looked deeply into my eyes, and told me I owed him at the very least a kiss for the nice breakfast I'd just enjoyed at his expense. I thanked him for the breakfast but told him "no thank you" to the kiss. As I started to open the car door, he viciously grabbed me, pulling me across the bench seat until I was practically sitting in his lap. Then Randy forced his mouth on mine so harshly that either his or my teeth bit into my lip, breaking the skin. I was terrified. My heart was pounding. Blood was oozing from my torn lip. Tears were streaming down my face. With all my strength, I shoved him away and bolted from his car as he screamed profanities at me.

My hands were shaking so badly it took what seemed like an eternity to find my keys, unlock the door, and scramble inside. Too afraid to see if he was coming after me, I locked the door and throw the car in reverse. Luckily, no one was behind me. I drove away like a bat out of hell, making a promise to myself to never get in a stranger's car again. Never. Ever.

I was so scared but that incident was nothing like the next.

My hands are trembling but *I* know that *you* need to know the truth about date rape. Nearly every woman I've spoken to has experienced some form of sexual abuse by an acquaintance, a stranger, a relative, a date, a spouse, or an ex-spouse, so perhaps the telling of this incident will help someone to be brave enough to *not* let it slide and report it. Sometimes we make unwise decisions but that does not give another person the right to force something, anything, on us that we do not want.

Here goes. It's two a.m. at a nightclub, where I had been drinking and dancing all evening with Roger, a good-looking, clean-shaven, blue-eyed blond. I'd seen him at the club several times in the past so I felt pretty sure he was most likely trustworthy—right? As the lights came up on the dance floor, he pulled me close and said the night was too young, he didn't want it to end. He would, he said, invite me to his house but his parents were visiting from out of town and sleeping on the pull-out sofa in the living room. He doesn't want to wake them. How about if I let him follow me home for just one more drink? A charismatic voice, smoothly combined with a side of alcohol, and I stupidly agreed.

Please understand that I did not make a habit of bringing men home but, because he was just so damn sexy, my guard was down—everything about him screamed "*Keeper!*" I watched in my rearview mirror as he followed me home, and once inside I poured us a Jack Daniels on the rocks. The night was cold, his kisses hot, and we soon ended up in my bedroom.

I had told him before we left the nightclub that we would have to be very quiet because my teenage sons were sleeping in the next room. We silently undressed and at long last, I saw what his body looked like under his designer clothes. His gorgeously lean, muscular, bronzed body was perfection, to say the least. His chest was hairless, and then I realized his entire body was hairless, which I found a little alarming but not kick-him-out-of-the-house frightening. A man's got a right to shave his body if he wants to, right? He kissed me softly, whispering that he couldn't wait to be inside my body. We climbed on the bed.

Before I knew it, he had flipped me over and pulled my hips up high, forcing me onto my knees. He grabbed my hair with one hand, put his other hand over my mouth, and whispered into my ear what he was about to do to me. I bit his hand and hissed, *"No! Get off me!"* With a hideously evil tone in his voice, he whispered hotly, his breath suddenly smelling like the foul stink of a rank dungeon, "If you scream, your sons will come in and see you getting fucked in the ass. Is that what you want, you little bitch, you whore, you slut?"

My insides felt like they were being ripped out of me as the pounding of his body went on and on. Finally, I felt his body beginning to shudder and knew his climax was near.

I kept trying to push him off, but his strength was magnified by an unholy rage. His hand was crushing my mouth. Tears, mixed with mascara, poured down my terrified face as I pray to God to "Please, please make him stop, let it be over." A few final thrusts and his back arched as he released his profane semen into my body. His head thrashed, causing his blonde wig to fly across the room.

With the despicable act over, he pushed me to one side, pulled the covers up to his chin, and said goodnight. "Are you kidding me!!!" I didn't dare scream but my voice was vicious. "Get out! Get out *now*! If you leave right now, I won't call the police!"

He retorted, "It's your word against mine, bitch. You know you liked it."

I clutched the bedclothes around me as he got dressed. He leered at me one last time as he grabbed his wig off the floor and left. He left me bleeding, in pain, and shaken to the core.

Quietly sobbing, I could not stop berating myself for being so insanely naive. I had let this maniac in my *home!* Where my sons were asleep! How could I be so stupid? No one, no one must ever know. So, I told no one. Until now.

Should I have called the police? Most definitely, but I was ashamed of my behavior and felt it was partly my fault.

Years later, I learned this despicable excuse for a man was a serial rapist, that he had been caught, convicted, and sentenced to spend the rest of his life in prison. He had shaved his head and body in order not to leave any evidence. Sick bastard. I'm sure his fellow inmates appreciated having a man like him in their midst. I wish I could hear him begging them to stop like I begged that night.

Rape is shamefully prevalent in all neighborhoods. Rich, poor, middle class. Some men feel entitled to rape their wives, ex-wives, daughters, dates. Ladies *and* gentlemen, hear me when I say no one has the right to force themselves on you. *No one*. Each of us has the right to say no and to expect to be listened to. To respect your choice to say no to sex. So scream long and loud, my sisters and brothers, and report any kind of abuse to the police.

Late night sojourns to the bright lights and pulsing music of nightclubs ended that night and I resigned myself to being alone the rest of my life. There simply are no Prince Charmings waiting to sweep me off my feet. Strangers=fear and pain.

Lesson 15: Date rape is—absolutely, unequivocally—real.

Chapter 16. Louie, The Love of My Life

So here it is, two years after my divorce. I'd seen dozens and dozens of men wander in and out of my whirlwind life. I was ready to settle down once and for all, and get used to the idea of being alone. I'd lived through two horrible experiences, two Thanksgivings, two birthdays, two Christmases, two dateless New Year's Eves and Valentine's Days. I didn't mind spending holidays alone any more. And then suddenly, miraculously, the love of my life appeared like an answer to prayer.

Where, you ask? At the little beer and wine bar where my sister worked as a bartender. No band, no dance floor, it was just a quiet place to escape life and have a drink or two, or three or four, or five.

I wasn't looking for love. I just went to meet the people my sister, Linda, served, so I could put faces to the names of the people she was always talking (mostly gossiping) about. One by one she introduced me to each of the patrons: Sally, Dick, Margie, Rod, Ann, Trish, and then there he was, sitting at the end of the bar, looking literally like a gift from the gods, minus bow and gift card of course. Five-nine, dark, sexy, and as mysterious as a villain in a James Bond movie.

Louie. My sister said his name was Louie. Precocious Patty noticed and chimed in, "Ooooh, Louie-Lou-eye, I could rock his world for a couple of weeks! Please let's take him home with us."

"Down girl," I scolded her, "you know perfectly well we don't do that anymore. Now shut up and go to sleep." So Patty and I stayed a while, then went home to watch that new show on Fox, *America's Most Wanted,* and get ready for work the next day.

I forgot about Louie until a month later, when Linda asked if I remembered the good-looking guy who'd been at the end of the bar. Maybe. Patty shouted, "He's the dark sexy one. Dang, you are stupid, Diana. Say, yes you remember him!"

"Wait, yes, I do remember him," I said to Linda.

"Why?"

"He asked if you would be coming back to the bar any time soon," Linda said. She wanted me to come down that night but I was hesitant. I told her I'd be there the following Sunday. The week went by and now I was sitting at the end of the bar, nervously waiting for him to show up. After what seemed like forever (it was actually only ten minutes), he walked through the door and sat next to me. We had a drink—me, wine and him, beer—and he surprised me by asking me to join him for a late dinner at a nearby coffee shop.

The dinner was uneventful but pleasant. Afterward, we drove back to the bar for a nightcap. When Louie pulled up and stopped, he turned and asked me for a kiss. (Who asks for a kiss these days?) The kiss was long, and sensual, and we agreed that instead of going into the bar we would have a little more privacy at his place. He drove slowly with me following in my own car. For some reason, I felt safe with him. After all, my sister knew him well, and he was so different from the other guys I'd been with.

Once at his home, I did the seducing by walking out of the bathroom wearing nothing except my long-tailed cream-colored silk blouse. His mouth flew open and his eyes bulged, but he quickly recovered. He wasn't used to being with quite so bold a woman.

That night, Precocious Patty met her match in what Louie called his Mr. Happy. Each tried to outdo the other during our night of passion. Our bodies seemed made for each other. After filling my body with his, he looked down at me and said, "I could fall in love with you."

The lovemaking continued. A couple of hours later, he looked down at me again and breathlessly whispered, "I *have* fallen in love with you."

What followed were twenty-six fabulously tumultuous, wonderfully fulfilling years together, and I never once thought of all those men I had been with before him. The bad experiences of the past melted away, replaced by memories of him. Louie was my all, the love of my life, and our souls were bound together for eternity when we exchanged our wedding vows. We watched each other's sons grow into manhood, find loves of their lives, marry, and have children. Although not bound by blood, he was Grandpa, Opa, to my son's children, their champion, and he loved them more than words can say.

Life was perfect.

Lesson 16: When you find the love of your life, you have everything you need.

Chapter 17. And Then Louie Was Gone

On a beautiful summer day like any other in Southern California, this wonderful, amazing, loving man was taken from me—suddenly, unexpectedly, shockingly—when Louie inexplicably collapsed in our front yard. In the span of just one tiny second, I was transported from our delightfully perfect life into a living nightmare. It continued during the ambulance ride to the emergency room, culminating three days later in a hospital ward filled with brain-dead patients waiting to be taken off life support.

Each day, I sat with him and witnessed the kindness of the doctors and nurses who took great pains to address him by name, explaining everything they were doing. Taking his pulse, listening to his heart and lungs with their stethoscopes. Adjusting knobs on the equipment that was keeping him alive. Tears fell as I quietly shared with each nurse and doctor who this man—my husband, my Louie— was: Vietnam veteran, son, brother, father, grandfather, and beloved commander of the American Legion. After three days of holding him, rubbing his feet and his hands, kissing his forehead, and willing him to wake up—*please, please, please I cannot go on without you*—I had to let him go. He was taken off life support. As I watched him take his last breath, I begged God to be merciful and take me too.

The grandchildren were frightened that someone they loved so much could be taken from them in the blink of an eye. So, I assured them their grandfather would be their guardian angel forever, and paint the sunrise and the sunset to remind us he was always near. I promised them that his spirit would visit us on the wings of birds and insects. I put on a brave face during his funeral, memorial service, and burial at a national cemetery.

In reality, I was a shell of the person Louie had fallen in love with, and was inconsolable for the next two years. My world had stopped turning. I prayed every night that the angels would come for me in my sleep.

I lived near one of my sons and his family. They tried to help by including me in all aspects of their lives. Eating dinner with them each evening. Joining them for outings and vacations. Taking the grandkids to school and picking them up. When my daughter-in-law had surgery, I felt useful again, for a short time, by cooking family meals and doing their laundry. My perfectly normal grandmotherly life ended each day with me in bed whispering, "One day closer, my love. I'm one day closer to being with you."

Then one evening I felt the dark veil lift and realized I was not meant to die yet. That it was my duty to embrace life for my sons and their families, for my sisters, for my friends. They were still alive and they loved and missed me. I read somewhere that loved ones who are taken from us can experience life through our eyes and that it was cruel to them for us to stay inside and be sad. So I began to live and love and laugh, and it felt sweetly, unbelievably powerful. I realized I *am* still the master of my own destiny, and went outside to let the wind flow through my hair. To feel the warm sunshine on my face. Let cold snowflakes melt on my tongue. Take long drives alone to drink in the beauty of lush green meadows. See the bleak starkness of the desert. Witness the churning waves of the ocean. Escape to snow-capped mountains. My world was turning once again.

Lesson 17: When you lose the love of your life, your world stops turning.

Chapter 18. Steve Said, "Thank-Yew, Thank-Yewveramuch."

Two months after Louie's passing, I moved away from where he fell, in Redondo Beach, to our second home in Henderson, Nevada, and began the laborious chore of closing down his business, settling his estate, and preparing the Henderson house for sale—the house my husband had worked so hard to beautifully renovate for us to move into.

Once the sale of the house was finalized, I invited a good friend to come up and take any of my furniture to her daughter. The poor thing had just left an abusive husband, and she and her small daughter were sleeping in sleeping bags on the floor in a totally empty apartment. My friend was thrilled, and happy to drive a U-Haul truck from Los Angeles to Henderson to get the furniture. We spent the day loading up beds and the living room and dining room furniture.

When we finished, a change of clothes and fresh makeup were all we needed to get us in the mood for the drive to downtown Las Vegas for a nice dinner and to maybe catch a show, before my girlfriend left the next morning for the long drive back to Los Angeles. As luck would have it—well, actually I don't believe in "luck;" I believe our lives are guided and directed by a greater force—one of the show singers was MIA. Apologies from the other two singers in the trio were made. They said they were taking a break, assuring us that a call had gone out to a friend and he'd arrive shortly to join them. Then miracle of miracles—*Elvis was in the building*! Of course this was over thirty years since Elvis died, and it was Steve Connolly, an Elvis tribute artist, who, like Superman, came to save the day!

I let out a scream and sang along as Steve/Elvis belted out my most beloved Elvis songs. My girlfriend poked me in the ribs just in time for me to see him lift one eyebrow and saunter over, singing directly to me. He then gave me a lap dance I'll *never* forget. Yes, I instantly fell in love with this entertainer whose performance dried my tears and, for a little while, made me feel whole again. After the show, Steve thanked me for making his performance one that no one in attendance would ever forget.

A few months later, I returned to downtown Las Vegas and saw a poster advertising that Steve Connolly was performing his solo show, *The Spirit of the King,* at the casino where I had seen him. I bought a ticket and thoroughly enjoyed the show, again seeing him afterward. He actually thanked me for helping him get the solo gig. Management had been so impressed with his charisma with the audience (mainly me, sigh) that they brought him back several times, eventually hiring him as a solo act. He's been thrilling women and men of all ages five nights a week ever since.

Steve, you told me you were hoping you would be amongst the men I have loved in my book, and so now you know that yes, I will always love you—for singing to me that night and for making me realize that perhaps God is not finished with me on this earth, at least not just yet.

Lesson 18: <u>The Spirit of the King</u> is alive and well!

Chapter 19. Jimmying His Way into My Heart

While I was living the high life, going out dancing at the glitzy nightclubs of the eighties, I met Jimmy. Jimmy was tall, thin, handsome, a sharp dresser, and a fantastic dancer. We made a terrific dance duo and he would call every Monday night to let me know where that week's dance contests would be held. We drove all over Los Angeles County, almost always taking home a trophy or prize for our efforts. One night, I ended up back at his place for a late-night snack. One thing led to another. We ended up in bed expecting it to be like our performance on the dance floor— hot and sexy. But nothing. No sparks at all. Nada. This surprised us both, but instead of being embarrassed we laughed it off and decided that it was indeed better if we stayed "just friends."

I didn't realize what a good friend Jimmy was until the night he called to see what time he should pick me up for that night's dance contest. I regretfully informed him I was too ill, too miserable to even move, and explained that my misery would last for at least another twenty-four hours. He asked me what was wrong. I told him, "Endometriosis." Of course he'd never heard of it. Once I explained to my clueless bachelor friend what this strange-sounding, painful, recurrent disease meant to a woman, he immediately wanted to help. But I told him no, to go and have a good time without me. An hour later, my doorbell rang. There was Jimmy, big grin on his face, arms filled with bags. He had canceled his plans for the night, bought a perfect-for-not-feeling-so-hot dinner of wonton soup from a Chinese restaurant, a two-liter bottle of ice cold 7-Up at the local liquor store, and a bag of VHS movies he'd rented. All of this for me. In fuzzy slippers and bulky pink chenille robe. No make-up and mussed hair. He announced he was there to take care of me, all night long if needed. He put down the bags and gently steered me to a chair. After pulling out the sofa bed in my living room, off he went to find pillows and blankets, and that's where I spent one of the very best nights of my life.

After rummaging in the kitchen, Jimmy appeared with ice and glasses for the soda, bowls for the soup, and a box of soda crackers. After quite ceremoniously fluffing the pillows, he settled me, and then himself, onto the sofa bed and popped in one of the movies. After we finished eating, he cleared the dishes, sat up in the sofa bed and nestled me in his arms for the evening, thoughtfully pausing the tape when I needed to go to the bathroom after drinking all that 7-Up.

Never, ever have I felt as cared for as I did that night while lying in his arms. I let myself go. I was no longer the Mom or the professional executive assistant or the disco queen. I was the sickie being cared for by the most generous, sweetest man I have ever known, my dancing buddy, Jimmy. We lost touch long ago but I will never forget his generosity of time and spirit.

Fast-forward thirty years. It was seven p.m. on a Saturday evening, two years after my husband passed away. I was sitting in front of the television, already in my pj's, eating a bowl of soup for dinner off a T.V. tray, when I made a vow to never sit home alone on a Saturday night again. Or on a Thursday night. Maybe not Monday either. So the following week, as hard as it was, I got dressed, put on makeup, curled my hair, and went to a local casino sports bar to watch Thursday night football. I walked in with my heart pounding, found one open spot at the bar and asked the gentlemen to the right and left if the seat was taken. They both said no, please have a seat.

I ordered a Corona with lime and started playing video poker on the machine in front of me so my drinks would be free and, after winning hand after hand, the quiet gentleman on my right commented on how well I was doing. "My name's Brian," he said. "What's yours?"

"Diana. I'm a widow and tonight's my first night out since my husband passed away two years ago." Brian's long, silky reddish-blonde hair was in a ponytail that he'd pulled through the back opening of a baseball cap. His light, fuzzy beard and mustache were trimmed neatly, and his flannel shirt, jeans, and work boots labeled him a workingman. It proved true. He delivered lime to the mines in a big-rig and was quite adamant that he did *not* want a girlfriend. Not now. Not *ever* again. He'd *had* it with women. He and his dog Ruby were perfectly happy being alone. I explained I was definitely not looking for a relationship either. Just someone to talk to. And talk we did. For hours. An exchange of phone numbers ended the evening and we went our separate ways.

A couple months later, I received an unexpected call from Brian asking me to join him for a cup of coffee at a nearby java place. I quickly changed clothes, touched up my makeup and hair, all the while wondering what his intentions were. To my complete and delighted surprise, he presented me with an exquisite, gilt-edged journal he'd seen at a truck stop shortly after we met. He said he thought of me and the journey I was on, and felt I could use the journal to write down my thoughts while my heart healed. What a kind, sweet gesture by someone I barely knew and hadn't even kissed or slept with or anything! I thanked him profusely, and thus began a wonderfully platonic relationship that has lasted for years through Facebook, phone calls, texts, and, upon rare occasion, visits in person.

Yes, men and women can be "just friends," with all the benefits of a wonderful friendship without the complication of a sexual relationship. And you're reading this book because Brian's gift of a writing journal was the beginning of me discovering my love of storytelling.

Thank you, Brian. You did good.

Lesson 19: Can men and women be just friends, without benefits? They most certainly can.

Chapter 20. Gentle Glen

Shortly after meeting Brian, I began frequenting a lounge that featured local bands. Drinks were free if you sat at the bar and played poker machines. The seats were hard to come by. One Saturday night, I spotted an open seat next to a striking, rugged-looking middle-aged man whose name was, I would learn, Glen. Glen was solidly built, of average height, with curly auburn hair and a thick mustache. His flannel shirt, jeans, and work boots told me he was a hard-working man out for a couple beers and a little music. We chatted some that night and wound up seated next to each other, not exactly by accident I suspect, for several Saturdays in a row.

In late December, Glen asked what I wanted Santa to bring me that year. What should I tell him, I wondered. I was lonely and sad, and my birthday was the next day. So I decided to tell him the truth. "Tomorrow's my birthday and I'd ask Santa for a birthday kiss at midnight by a handsome young man. And I'd like that man to be you." He looked surprised and asked if I'd like to move to the sofa near the band, where we would be a little more comfortable. I spotted him sneaking peeks at his watch until finally midnight arrived. He took me in his strong arms, kissed me tentatively, then passionately, and surprised us both when he whispered in my ear, "I'd like to give you a lot more than a kiss." My eyes grow wide. He said, "Follow me home?"

My heart was pounding. I hadn't been with another man since my husband had passed away. Then I realized, oh my gosh I didn't plan for this. I'd showered but hadn't shaved my legs in days. Would he throw up his hands in disgust and order me out of his home for such a dastardly and wanton lack of personal hygiene? Well, I'd find out, I guess! He took my hand while we nearly skipped out of the casino, giggling all the way. When I told him, I felt like a high school girl sneaking off with the star football player, he threw his head back, laughing, and said, "So do I." That night, he woke Precocious Patty from her long, long nap and helped me remember how good it felt to be with a man. I will forever be grateful to Glen for his gentle, passionate re-introduction to the long dormant sexual side of my life.

The man had unbelievable stamina and we enjoyed each other's bodies literally all night long. In the early morning light, we agreed that although the night had been pretty amazing this was still just a *friendship*. No strings. Neither of us was ready for a commitment as girlfriend and boyfriend. Or is it woman friend and man friend? What the heck do you call it when you're both over fifty?

My love, my husband, had been gone two years and Glen's beloved wife had died two years before my Louie. Glen was fifty, and I was sixty-six, and the age difference didn't matter. We became best friends, spending most of our time together going out to dinner, on long rides in his truck, to the movies, fundraisers. And we made love. A lot. We remained best friends with benefits until I moved away—after which he almost instantly fell in love (actually, it did take him all of *four days*) with a woman his own age. They were married just recently, and I really do wish them the best. But I truly miss his friendship. He is no longer allowed to have any contact with past girlfriends or friends who are girls (especially me). You know there's more to the story but I don't want to be really catty and I could. Oh, I definitely could *(meow)*.

Lesson 20: Friends with benefits are sometimes a downright necessity.

Chapter 21. The Man from Long Ago

According to family legend, my great-grandfather on my father's side was quite a guy, so maybe that's where I get the untraditional side of my personality. He traveled around the Wild West as a land assayer, working for seven years in one area and then moving on to the next. The story goes that he left a wife and family back in Kansas. However, Great-grandpa missed his family so much that he would set out to find an eligible young woman to marry in each new town he moved to. Yep, he would woo her, marry her, and leave her and any and all offspring born to them seven years later, when he moved on to the next assigned town. One of the women he married was my great-grandmother, who was, I'm told, half Cherokee, half Blackfoot. So apparently, I've got a trace of Native American in my blood. But I never really thought about it much, until something magical happened during a Native American ceremony at a show in Buena Park, California.

I was there with my family, celebrating my dad's birthday, when Native Americans dressed in ceremonial feather headdresses and soft moccasins began to gather on stage. Slow, methodical drumming was accompanied by soft chanting. A handsome young man wearing leather shirt and pants appeared in the center. His striking headpiece of long white feathers draped nearly to the floor. To the beat of the drums, the young man slowly began dancing around a bonfire in the center of the stage.

The sound of the pounding drums called to me, drawing me into another world of long ago. I was a small girl sitting at the edge of the group, watching my big brother as he danced and twirled, mesmerized at the sight of him. Just that afternoon he had held me high and I laughed and laughed as he twirled me round and round. Tremendous pride at the man he was becoming welled up inside my tiny body. Too soon my brother's voice fell silent and, as the final drum note faded, I felt a strong pull as my body raced through a dark tunnel toward a bright, white light. Suddenly, I was seated once again with my family.

My body was weak and my mind felt fuzzy. I asked the rest of my family if anything strange happened to them during the performance. "No, why?" they asked. My son Robbie laughed as he said that *I* was the only thing strange in the room. So now I knew. I was the only one in my family blessed with a private experience.

After we returned home, I researched the phenomena and spoke to an expert on Native American history. He assured me I had most likely experienced an *ancestor's memory* hidden deep in my brain. This type of memory can be triggered by a sight or sound similar to what the ancestor felt at the time the memory was made. It's genetic. Similar to the urge a bird feels when it is time to fly south for the winter even though there are no other birds of its kind around—it does what its ancestors did. It flies south.

Hoping to recapture the feeling, I've tried a number of times to duplicate the experience that triggered the memory, but have failed each time. I've given up trying and accepted that it was a rare and magical one-time experience.

Lesson 21: Genetic memories are magically unplanned and impossible to duplicate.

Chapter 22. Grazie, Grazie, Giuseppe and Gino!

My bucket list had long included a trip to Italy but after my husband was gone, I feared I might never get to see the country I longed for from watching romantic movies and the travel channel. Then one day, my nineteen-year-old granddaughter offered to go with me. I immediately said *yes*.

As the date of departure arrived, we were very excited about the trip, even after a rough beginning. Delayed by a rare rainstorm in Los Angeles, we missed our flight out of New York by thirty minutes—at a cost of $800 in "missed flight" fees. But, what could we do? We found a room for the night near the JFK airport, ordered in Chinese food at one a.m. (Who knew New York City was famous for late night foods-to-go deliveries?) We had arranged a late checkout, slept until noon, then stayed in bed in our pj's watching movies until it was time to leave for the airport late in the afternoon.

We allowed ourselves several hours at the airport, just to be sure we were on time for the ten-p.m. flight, so we ate dinner at one of the airport restaurants and then had an uneventful, smooth flight. Landing in Milan, a brand-new white Mercedes waited for us. We drove off the rental lot and, with my granddaughter's cell phone GPS, found our way to the expressway. Our final destination, a hotel in the quaint town of Montecatini, was a "mere" five-hour drive away. It was early afternoon, so no problem. And away we go!

Within ten minutes, it started raining. Raining like crazy. I finally figured out how to turn on the windshield wipers, only to have a warning light pop up on the dashboard. In, of course, Italian. We found a pullout on the highway where we could stop, and turned on the four-way flashers. Thank goodness for Google translates: the warning signal was telling us "low tire pressure front passenger side." Okay, that was a simple fix. We just needed to find a gas station, right? Again, the Internet to the rescue! Google helped us locate a nearby town with several *stazioni di servizio*. Driving cautiously, we arrived, and after so many turns on roundabouts that I felt like we were on a virtual merry-go-round, we reached the first gas station. It was closed. And so was the next, and the next. Are you kidding me? It was the middle of a Friday afternoon, where was everyone!!! We pulled into the fourth gas station and by then immediately recognized the *Chiuso* sign hanging in the window, announcing it too was closed. Not again! Had the entire region run out of gas or what?

Just then a small truck pulled up. With my English-to-Italian translation book clutched tightly in my hand, I nearly pounced on the poor driver. There I was, frantically flipping pages and pleading for help in probably the worst Italian ever, because the man could not understand a single word I was saying. Out of desperation, I grabbed his hand and nearly dragged him to the passenger side of my car. I pointed at the flat tire, then turned both palms up in the international sign for "What can I do?"

Finally, communicating without words is a success! This gentle workingman, in greasy clothes and dirty hair, fished a huge key ring, filled with more keys than I've ever seen, out of his ridiculously baggy pants pocket. After trying key after key, the garage door opened and he dragged out a huge air pump. By then another man had joined him, both speaking rapid Italian, gesturing toward us. Big smiles were on their faces. It seemed they'd deduced we were damsels in distress, in need of them as knights in shining armor. Our sense of relief was immense as the men attached the air hose and the tire began to inflate. And again, big smiles from our two heroes, Giuseppe and Gino.

Soon the tire pressure was perfect and these delightful men had rescued us from our dilemma. Giuseppe wildly gestured for the translation book still clutched in my hands. He found the phrase "Everything's okay now," grinned like a Cheshire cat, and asked for ten dollars in Euros. With great relief we paid him, giving both men big hugs before setting on our way once again. We glanced back and saw the men laughing and waving their hands in huge half circles over their heads. I don't think I have ever been so grateful for anything in my life as I was for these sweet Italian knights in grease-stained armor.

Once we were safely back on the road, I finally realized why all the stations were closed. Everything was, not just the service stations. It was siesta time! Every business day, from one to four o'clock, all Italian shops and businesses close for a "siesta." Apparently, the tradition began decades ago when workers came in from the fields and factories, banks and shops during the heat of the afternoon, and went home to have a nice lunch. After eating, they would fall asleep for a couple hours, then, energized from the meal and nap, returned to finish the day's work.

There's a little twist on how the afternoon nap started in France. Business owners who traveled more than an hour from their homes in the suburbs to conduct business in the city did not have time for a round trip home for lunch. So they solved the problem by acquiring a local mistress at whose apartment they enjoyed lunch, a little rendezvous between the sheets, a nap, and then back to work until dusk. Who knows where the truth lies, but I prefer this "ooh la la" version.

Lesson 22: You don't need to speak the same language to communicate.

Chapter 23. Outnumbered by Noah

It started out innocently enough. I called my seventeen-year-old grandson Noah to find out what he'd like for Christmas. Since baseball was his passion and he was on his high school's varsity baseball team, as well as in a travel league, he was always asking for specific baseball equipment, but this time was different. He hesitantly asked me for money to go toward buying a used pickup truck. I asked him how much he had saved so far and he admitted he didn't have a single penny saved as yet but would start by saving all or at least most of his Christmas money.

I thought to myself, this child needs a goal to maximize his savings efforts or else he's going to end up with $12.37 saved by next summer. So, like the good grandma I am, I issued a challenge. "Tell you what. I will match every dollar you save between now and your birthday on July fourteenth. The matching dollars will be your Christmas, graduation, and birthday gifts." When Noah eagerly agreed, I asked him to text or call me at the beginning of each month with how much he had saved so I would know whether to get a part-time job, ha-ha. How much could he save, right, a few hundred at most?

January 1st came and he reported his savings were at $400. Okay that's Christmas money, it should slow way down after this.

February 1st the amount had increased to $1,400. What? He saved $1,000 in a month!!! What is he, a drug dealer for crying out loud? Or perhaps he robbed the liquor store down the street? So I get on the phone and talk to his dad, my son Bob (formerly Robbie, who at sixteen announced to me that he preferred to be called Bob). I wanted to find out how the heck this seventeen-year-old kid had saved so much money in one month while going to school full time. Bob proudly informed me Noah took my challenge very seriously and, on his own had found a job. Two, in fact. Noah was working as a laborer for a construction company on the weekends making $15 an hour, plus flipping burgers after school three nights a week for minimum wage.

Are you kidding me, I thought. He's really gotten into this challenge! And he'd told his dad that with me matching his savings it was like he was getting paid double— half from his paychecks, half later from me for his truck. Damn, that kid was smart! Maybe, I hoped, he'd quit the jobs when he figured he's saved enough for a cheap, clunky little truck. Fingers crossed!

By March 1st he was at $2,400. Uh oh, this could cost me big time! I talked to my son again, who was really proud of his son. Understandably so! Noah had learned to weigh the benefits and the costs before he spent *any* money. Whether it was worth it, because spending would end up costing him double, since the money he spent wouldn't be matched by me. Tickets to a concert with his girlfriend? Way too much, so he rents a movie and they watch it at home. Clothes? Nope. He can do without until after his birthday in July. Yikes!

April 1st and I hear the ding on my cell phone announcing a text message from grandson. I don't want to see what it says! I wait three hours to open it. He's *only* at $3,000, thank God! He had quit the construction job. I look skyward, please Lord, help me on this one! Maybe Noah would quit the burger job to study for finals?

I eagerly await May 1st. He has $3,400. Whew! Prom had cost him a pretty penny, hallelujah!

June 1st arrives and I'm planning my trip to attend graduation. He's at $3,600 and graduates in three weeks. How much more can he save in three weeks? Grandson then reminds me the challenge is until his birthday in mid-July. *Groan*!!!

I braced myself for the final total on July 14. Oh my goodness! $5,400!!!

Noah not only continued to flip burgers after quitting the construction job, he offered to paint his family's house, undercutting the lowest labor bid by the contractors by $1,200, and hired a friend to help him. The friend offered to work for free—how good a kid is that? —so Noah would have more for me to double, but my grandson stuck to his fair play guns and insisted on paying him. Noah still cleared a small bundle.

Oh my lord, I had planned on $3,000 max and now look what happened. Why hadn't I put a cap on how much I'd match? There went the cruise I had hoped to take. And going to that new restaurant for a steak and lobster dinner. Even the new purse I had my eye on. But you know, I can't tell you how proud I am for the way this man-child had taken the challenge to heart and looked at every angle to get the most out of it. Truthfully, he was very fair about it, too. His dad—*my traitor son*—even told Noah to count his graduation money gifts and that could be another few hundred dollars toward the total, but Noah said no, that wasn't fair. He had not earned that money, they were gifts. Thank God the boy has scruples!

We agreed the final amount to be matched would be $5,400. With the $5,400 he had saved, plus graduation money and $5,400 from me, Noah had just over $12,000. Wow!

His parents and friends helped him look, long and hard, for the best pickup truck for a just-graduated-from-high-school-just-turned-18-year-old. His heart was set on a full-size truck with a *big* engine, and he finally found the perfect vehicle. A mighty fine dark gray, 2007 Ford 150 XLT SuperCrew with 127,000 miles and a V8 engine. Lousy mileage but great for the ego. And quite an accomplishment, considering he'd had zero dollars saved just seven months earlier. That truck is his baby, his pride and joy.

Noah learned a number of life lessons from the challenge. How rewarding it is to work hard toward a goal. The pride he felt when he accomplished that goal. How fulfilling, how thrilling, it is to watch your savings grow, instead of living paycheck to paycheck. How much more he appreciates the truck because his own blood, sweat, and tears went into saving money to buy it. To ponder each purchase's worth before spending the money. Good lessons for any teenager. Heck, good lessons for anyone at any age to learn.

Noah's grandma—me—learned a couple of very valuable lessons, too. Be careful when you issue a challenge. Always set a cap on anything to do with money. Never, *ever* underestimate your own grandchildren: they have the same blood running through their veins as you do, and will always figure out a way to fully maximize an opportunity.

Kudos to you, Noah. This grandma's thrilled to have been part of your lesson.

Lesson 23: Be careful when you issue a challenge.

Chapter 24. Under Adam's Fig Leaf

Not very long ago, I visited a friend in a small town in northern Nevada. While there, Diane introduced me to a friend of hers. Adam, she told me, was a sweet man whose wife of eighteen years, the mother of his two sons, had shattered his idyllic world by callously announcing to him that she no longer loved him, had been having an affair with another man, and wanted a divorce. Diane, Adam, and I had dinner together. He had graying hair, a full beard, and wore the uniform-of-the-day in a Wild West mining town—plaid flannel shirt, jeans, and work boots. Adam and I were instantly attracted to each other and seemed to possess what the other needed. His heart was breaking and he needed the solace of a woman's arms; I had not been with a man for quite a while and needed, well, a *man's touch*, if you get my drift.

Adam and I spent a fun, sexy dinner together, outrageously flirting and feeding each other while Diane bemusedly looked on from across the table. Keep in mind this man was thirty years younger than me. Oh, and he was short! Barely taller than me, at five-feet-five inches. I'd never been with a "height-challenged" man before, and as the night wore on, I begin to wonder if the rumors about the relevance of a man's stature in regard to certain other sizes of his were true.

We walked out to the parking lot and necked in my car while deciding the next step in this relationship. His kisses were long and passionate and I could see by the growing bulge in his pants that he was as excited as I was. We went for a drive and ended up in my hotel room. (I know, you're shocked, right?) I went into the bathroom to "freshen up" and came out just in time to see Adam taking off his jeans. The rest of his clothing had been hastily piled in the middle of the floor. Then he dropped his drawers and I nearly fainted. This handsome man's hard, perfect body was like a Greek god's, an un*believably* endowed Greek god. I'm talking halfway down his thigh (yeah, yeah, his thigh was not all that long but still). Precocious Patty lit up like a light bulb and begged me to get started. *Now*, she shouted. I told her we needed to be gentle with Adam because he was recovering from a broken heart. Maybe he wasn't up to being with us. Patty didn't care if *he* was ready, she was, right *now*. Patty and I asked him if he'd like to get more comfortable. On the bed. Quickly he unclothed me, adding my stuff to the pile of his stuff on the floor. A little more kissing and a bit of giggling before jumping on the bed, and beginning the first grand exploration of each other's bodies…

As we lay basking in the afterglow of a very long and heated exchange of bodily fluids, I asked Adam to compare his hand to mine. I expected to find big hands because of his, you know. To my surprise, his hand was the same size as mine—and I have pretty small hands. I looked down at

123

his size eight feet and mumbled to myself, "Apparently it's not true."

Unfortunately, I said it just loud enough for him to hear, because he indignantly sat straight up in bed. "No, it's not true! Why does every woman think the size of a man's hands and feet has anything to do with a man's, umm, private parts?" he exclaimed. "I've been putting up with stupid remarks my entire life and I'm sick of it!" he bellowed.

He simmered down before he continued. "Like the women at work. Every time I walk in the office at the mine, they just cannot resist telling me how cute I am but they could never go for me. I'm too short, and have tiny hands, and feet, and you know what *that* means. Giggle giggle. *Not* funny. No, they don't know what '*that* means' and I bet their men aren't all that big down there anyway, I don't care how tall they are! I want to show them it's not true but I can't. I'd get fired. So I have to keep my mouth shut and listen to them giggle." Dejectedly, he lay back down and crossed his arms over his chest.

It didn't take much enticing by me, though, before we were back to the fun part of sharing a hotel room. At least for a while, we both forgot about his crushed ego.

Those women are fools. They don't know the truth, but oh boy, do I know. And I'm certain that as his broken heart begins to heal, there'll be a lot more women discovering the truth about this height-challenged young man in the prime of his life. Like a two-carat diamond ring inside a tiny velvet ring box, sometimes good things do come in small packages. So don't judge a box by its wrapping, a book by its cover, or a man by his height. Or the size of his hands or feet for that matter.

Whew, I gotta take a break. Just thinking about this guy…settle down, Patty, he's five hundred miles away!

Lesson 24: Sometimes, big things come in small packages.

Lesson 24a: After finishing this chapter, I did a little more research about the dilemma of probable size. The latest theory, when attempting to determine the size of a man's private parts before moving a relationship forward to the intimate stage, is to carefully look at his fingers. Fingers? Yes, his fingers. Hold his hand in yours and run your finger along each finger. Not only is this highly erotic to the man, for you to be so fascinated by his fingers, but it gives you a chance to check the length of his ring finger in relation to the length of his index finger. These are the first and third fingers, not the middle one which should be the longest for obvious reasons of pleasuring a woman. If the man's ring finger is longer than his index finger, his male member is most likely larger than normal. If the ring finger is shorter than the index finger then he might be a little on the small side. I've tested this theory on a few men and so far, it seems to be pretty accurate. Now it's your turn to do a little investigating of your own. Feel free to contact me with your own research. The results so far have been fascinating!

Chapter 25. Barry and Chaz, Bombast and Chaos

Personally, I give everyone the benefit of the doubt and will put up with a lot before love turns to loathe. But unfortunately, it can and it has and it may happen again. To be absolutely truthful, though, there are no *human beings* I truly loathe. I know there are psychological elements and sometimes personal demons involved in inappropriate, loathsome behavior so I suppose I should say it's certain *behaviors* I have learned to loathe, thus loathing the vessel that spews them.

Behaviors I loathe include, but are not limited to, racism, sexism, homophobia, rudeness, arrogance, bullying, insensitivity, cruelty, and unkindness. In my never-to-be-humble opinion, there is absolutely no need for any of these behaviors by anyone, ever. Period. If a behavior is not intended to uplift another person or situation it cannot and must not be tolerated. And really, unkindness covers it all.

Let me explain what I'm trying to say. Take Barry, an enigmatic business executive who seemed to have everything a woman could want. Good looking, wore expensive clothes and shoes. Had a company limo, driver, and bodyguard with him at all—and I mean *all*—times. Beautiful home with servants. But all of this came with a terrible attitude in his private life. Barry's public persona was very professional, but when we were alone out would come his aggression and hatred for minorities. According to him, some races are lazy liars. Others are deceitful and will steal you blind. Immigrants will say anything to get you to marry them and then slowly import all their relatives to live with and off you. The longer I knew him the more often his racist rantings occurred. I tried reasoning with him about his opinions but to no avail. Finally, my admiration of his success in business turned to loathing because of his bigoted remarks.

One evening, I cringed inwardly when Barry announced to me that he was considering running for governor. One of his minions recommended he go for it. Live in a big mansion, maybe be president of our great country one day. Dear God, *no*! Then that notion was soon abandoned, as he pondered what it would take to become a minister and start his own non-profit church. Good lord, how could he possibly think he possessed any of the traits for either of these professions? Needless to say, he was soon just another chapter in my book and the further away I get from this magnetic nut ball, the better I feel.

Dishonesty is another one of my pet peeves. Anyone who does not tell the truth does not deserve the time of day from me. I must admit that I'm occasionally blinded by a man's personality and cannot tell if he's truthing or lying. Or I just don't want to think he's lying. Case in point, Chaz. Chaz is an attractive man in his late sixties with a full head of gray hair, neatly trimmed mustache, and goatee. Boasts a nice, healthy tan so he must have a pool, I surmise. Oooh, about five-eleven, two hundred pounds, all of it of middle-aged man candy. We met at a lounge one evening and had a lovely conversation. Exchanged phone numbers and occasionally texted or spoke on the phone. His wife had died a few months earlier so he was still grieving. And lonely. Chaz missed the companionship of a good woman, and apparently my personality reminded him of his late wife. Finally, he asked me out to dinner but the depth of his feelings frightened him; he asked me not to be hurt but said he wasn't ready for a relationship just yet. So I backed off and started dating someone else. Barry to be specific.

Couple months down the road I get a text. It's Chaz. He had seen me with Barry a few times and asked if I was still seeing him. Yes, why, I ask. He doesn't text back but two minutes later my phone rings. It's Chaz. "I need to speak to you openly," he says. "I saw Barry with another woman the other night. I hope you don't mind me telling you but in my opinion his behavior was inappropriate if he's still seeing you." I inform Chaz that Barry and I do not have an exclusive relationship so he's free to see whomever he wishes. Chaz asks if he could call me again and perhaps go on a date. Sure, I tell him, thinking to myself I was ready to dump the racist jerk Barry anyway.

Two days later, Chaz is on the phone again. Texting turns into sexting and before long we are hot and heavy for each other. We begin spending the night together. Sex is unbelievable. Soon we're spending most of our time together. Sharing stories. Lots of stories about the men and women we'd been with. One day, Chaz confides in me that he loves chaos. I could tell by his messy, chaotic bedroom that he liked things in disarray, so I let it go without further thought. Then one day he tells me he can't see me anymore.

He wants to bed another woman. Needs his batteries charged by the excitement of the chase. Okay, that's over. Oh well, it was fun while it lasted. Couple weeks later, Chaz tells me she was not a nice lady and he isn't going to date her any more. Wants to see me again. Why not? We were great together. Then it happens again a few weeks later. Another woman he wants to get in her pants. Really? And this one's way older than him? Go for it you old fool, I tell him. Just leave me out of it. Oh no, he assures me, once this is over, I'll be ready to settle down. With you. Like an idiot, I believe him. I can see you rolling your eyes. Yes, I know now that I was totally and completely blindsided by this guy.

Then Chaz asked me to come to his home for a party. A barbecue with a few friends. He said his new girlfriend would be there, and I said no way. I'd seen her. She was no prize. Chaz texted me again, the morning of the barbecue, with the full menu. Steak, lobster, shrimp. Tempting. So I went. Let's just say his new girlfriend and I did not get along. She was an uptight, unattractive old *beyotch* and I must admit I was more than a little catty to her. I saw Chaz laughing in the kitchen as he prepared the meat for the barbecue but thought nothing of it.

In spite of the friction between Chaz and me, regarding his poor choice in a girlfriend, we stayed uneasy friends. I couldn't figure out why he so desperately wanted me in his life but I enjoyed being with him. I admit it, I cared about this big lug of a guy. But then I finally figured him out. The whole chaos thing kept eating at the back of my mind until a light bulb went on. Chaz had orchestrated the clash, the chaos, the pandemonium caused by his proclivities for dating new women while keeping me in his life. He loved to see me in pain. To create chaos in my life. He had played me the whole time. Chaz was an evil, despicable man and I hated him. Loathed him. So I told him exactly what I thought of him. His explanation? He liked chaos! I told him to shove chaos up his ass and never speak to me again. The end.

"Do unto others as you would have them do unto you" is the Golden Rule to live by. Well, unless you're a masochist, leave the cat o' nine tails in your bedroom when you go out in public and play nice with your fellow human beings.

Bottom line: if you want to be a friend or lover of mine, do not exhibit any of the aforementioned behaviors or I will drop you faster than a hot potato on a hot summer's night. Now that that bit of ugliness is out of the way, let's move on to something lots more fun to talk about. Like revenge— *bwah-ha-ha*.

Lesson 25: Love can turn to loathe when reality sets in.

Chapter 26. Back Atcha, Benny!

Revenge is a rather harsh concept, but befits occasions in which you have been treated in an extremely unfair manner. Indeed, if you wait long enough the time will eventually come that downright welcomes, sometimes even *begs*, you to exact a non-lethal, non-violent form of revenge. Let me tell you about a recent act of revenge that I assure you, dear reader, you will relish.

One of my "human dildos," who would be far better off learning to control his acidic comments about people in general and a few of my dear friends—Benny the Jet, of course—was constantly berating other races and, in particular, the "class" of people I personally associate with. They were below Benny's social status, as he was an executive at a rather large casino whose job included catering personally to high rollers, clients that spent upward to a half million dollars at his hotel. We'd been seeing each other for a couple of months, during which I had been extremely accommodating to the demands of his position.

Benny called me one day after a doctor's appointment, quite distraught. He'd been diagnosed with an ailment that may or may not be fatal. I was very supportive, offering to make chicken soup, take him to his appointments, anything really that he needed. But Benny let me know in no uncertain terms that he was surrounded by an inner circle of adoring friends and employees who would be seeing to his every need, but that he could still see me for more intimate desires, upon rare occasion. He hadn't done very well serving my "intimate" needs for some time so I wasn't terribly broken up at this turn of events. I asked him to stay in touch, to which he said most definitely he would. That I was by far the best lay he'd ever had, and he refused to give me up as long as his body continued to draw breath. Lucky me.

After treatment failed to correct his health issue, which by now he'd labeled as probably an incurable blood cancer, Benny arranged to fly to New York for a second opinion and treatment, if available. On his way to the airport, he telephoned me to unexpectedly tick off the vast number of reasons that he should no longer see me: 1: I had researched him online to confirm his identity, which was to him an unbelievably rude invasion of privacy (even though it was my feeling that I was merely protecting myself from any scam artists). 2: My current band of friends' social status was far beneath his. 3: The places I chose to frequent were (here I could picture him pursing his lips and shaking his head) just unacceptable for someone of his status to be seen in. Blah, blah, blah.

I let him finish and retorted with statements that the only friends I'd ever seen him with were of the same class as my friends. For example, his disgusting driver/bodyguard. His two former girlfriends—one a beautician working illegally out of her house, the other a flight attendant, neither hardly what you'd call upper crust. That he loved to sing karaoke at a nightclub where he had to wear a concealed gun because of the bad area and clientele. I concluded by stating, in no uncertain terms, that my assessment of his life and friends was pretty damned low and he had some nerve trying to make me feel bad about mine.

Benny listened quietly during my tirade, then wearily told me he didn't want to fight any more and would call when he got to New York. Hours go by, then days, weeks, and months and still no word from him.

I was left to assume, a) his plane disappeared on the way to New York, possibly abducted by aliens, b) he died on the way to or at the airport, or c) he was a jackass, and I should be relieved he was out of my life. I left one text and one voice mail, both of which went unanswered, and then gleefully resumed my former life with my low-life friends, sans one fancy executive. I completely forgot about him until his birthday came up on my phone's calendar. After some hesitation, I decided to be the bigger person and call to leave him a message saying I hoped he is still alive and wishing him a very happy birthday.

I dialed the number, it rang and rang, and just before it transferred to voicemail a very flustered-sounding Benny answered. "Hello Diana. I've been meaning to call you. I had a heart attack, sort of. It turned out it to be angina and they hospitalized me for three weeks in New York, then transferred me to a facility in Florida for five weeks to recuperate and I just got back in town last week," he exclaimed breathlessly in one run-on sentence. "How have you been?"

I knew he was lying like the rag rug on my grandmother's back porch, so I innocently replied, "I've been just fine. When I didn't hear back from you, I assumed you were dead and that's what I've been telling everyone who asked about you."

Silence for a moment on the other end of the phone while he digested this shocking conclusion of mine. Then he said, "Really? You told people I'm dead? Didn't you check the obituaries?"

"Of course I checked the obituaries but assumed no one cared enough about you to announce your death in the paper," I said rather cold-heartedly.

"Wow," Benny said. "Umm, so what have you been doing since I left?"

"Oh, I was at my beach house in Redondo Beach for a few weeks, then came back to work on my latest book." In actuality, I had only *rented* a beach house for a week, for my son's fiftieth birthday party. "I'm almost finished with my book and it will be coming out in a few months."

"You're a writer?" Benny asked.

"Oh yes. If you had ever given me a chance to get a word in edgewise during your totally self-involved conversations, I would've told you," I said, a tad self-righteously. "I own homes all over the world. I'm worth far more than any of your big-shot clients, and my latest book is a memoir of my life."

And then he asked, seductively, "Am I in it, as the best lover you've ever had?"

I laughed out loud. "Good lord, no. You're mentioned a couple of times. As worth nothing more than a human dildo and that you're a self-serving egomaniac. My greatest lover gets several chapters. A quickie to him lasts ninety minutes.

You, more like none. I've known him for a number of years and his turn was next in my stable when you disappeared."

"You have a stable?" he squeaked, then added, "Am I in your stable?"

"Of course I have a stable, but no you are not in it. I call it my Stud Stable. It's a list of the greatest lovers in my life. When I stop seeing one man, I move to the next one on the list."

"I want to be on the list," he exclaimed.

"No, no, my friend. My studs must be completely trustworthy. I know you're lying right now because my 'people' saw you at a casino a few weeks ago. You were hanging out with several lowlifes, laughing and acting like a big shot. You were *not* in Florida recuperating. And *my* stud stable is available to me at a moment's notice. As an account executive, *you* are a literal slave to your clients, and that precludes you from availability to me," I responded with a generous helping of contempt in my voice.

Although initially stunned, Benny recuperated quickly and tried to entice me with a promise he'd make time for me the following week, even though I was, of course, below his social standing. I curtly cut him off, "Apparently you weren't listening to me, Benny. I know exactly what you're saying. I cannot tell you how difficult it was for *me* to date *you* since you are so far below me socially and economically. Even though you were fun for a while, I cannot risk being seen with you, a glorified butler to the sorta rich and barely famous."

The conversation ended with him again asking, nay *begging*, permission to be placed "even at the bottom" of my Stud Stable list and to please, please call him in the future when his name came up. I told him it was doubtful I'd ever reach his name because the lovers ahead of him were far superior, but you never know. He's number thirteen, not a very lucky number.

Did he see it coming? Absolutely not. Benny had no clue I was lying outrageously to make him feel the betrayal and humiliation he had so callously dealt to me. Now he knew what it felt like to be treated with contempt. The tables had turned. He hung up with a deflated ego and the aching, burning desire to somehow, some way, someday be allowed back in my life.

Not a chance, you lying little bastard, not a chance in hell you'll ever see me again. Go wiggle on your belly because you are nothing but a lowly worm to me.

Although I do have to thank him for one thing: After I hung up on Benny the Jet, I felt like the Diana O'Donnell Moreno of yesteryear. Confident. Powerful. Beautiful. So for that, I thank you, Benny.

Now, on to my favorite subject.

Lesson 26: Revenge is a dish best served cold.

Chapter 27. Kindle Is a Verb, Not a Device

Sex can be as crude as the rutting of mindless animals in a dark, garbage-strewn alley or as transcending as an out of body experience. All some may want is the quick sexual release and that is certainly your prerogative, but as for me, I want to be *transcended*. I want to feel my body, my mind, and my soul come alive in the hands of another. To ultimately reach the final crescendo of a mind-blowing orgasm as I'm transported to another level of consciousness. Is your heart rate increasing just thinking about it? My dear reader, I hope so. Mine is.

First and most importantly, you must understand that lovemaking shouldn't just *happen* on the spur of the moment. That's just sex. Making love means one must take the time to be totally and completely immersed. Not just in the other person's body, but their consciousness. This is not a simple task. Creating time in the midst of our hectic schedules is becoming a lost art form because of the seduction of electronic devices. Yes, seduction. These *things* want to rule our lives. Cell phones, iPads, the Internet, Facebook, Twitter, television, video games, YouTube and videos constantly beckon us to spend time with *them*. Like the sirens of ancient days, they reach inside our minds. *You need us. You cannot manage your life without us. What if someone calls? Or texts? What if you get an important email that your bank account is running dangerously short of funds? Your child gets sick at school. Your mother needs a ride to the emergency room. Wait, look! —your favorite movie of all time is now streaming on Roku.* So you acquiesce and pick up that device. And suddenly, it's three hours later. Work starts in five hours. I better get to sleep. I should have spent that time making love. Too late now. Tomorrow, I'll be a better spouse tomorrow.

None of the aforementioned electronic devices can operate at all without batteries or a charging station. Sex doesn't need either (unless, of course, you prefer certain, umm, "personal toys" in order to have a fully romantic session). Your full attention is all that's required to make the other person (and *you*) soar to unknown, unexplored, unimaginable heights of ecstasy. Makes me want to head out right now and bring my lover in for a little soaring. How about you?

So put down whatever it is that's distracting you (yes, even this book! It'll wait) and vow to expend as much time and effort on making love to the *person* you care about as you put into those soulless *things* that want to dominate your life. Vow to become that one person remembered for your talents until the end of time. That's what I learned from that one truly great lover who makes both Precocious Patty and I quiver just *thinking* about him.

Lesson 27: A great lover makes love to the body, mind, and soul.

Chapter 28. Waiting on Joaquin

Like a hot, steamy romance novel, we met on a summer night inside an air-conditioned cocktail lounge. Joaquin was his name. Mid-sixties. Light conversation was followed by dancing cheek to cheek, drinking in the scent of each other's bodies. Suddenly it's last call. He takes my hand in his as we walk to retrieve our cars at the valet station. I notice Joaquin's hands and feet are very large for his average height of about five-eleven. The seductive chivalry of our walk is slightly intoxicating, even to a woman like me who thought I'd seen it all. As my car pulls up, I impulsively give Joaquin a warm, full body hug and quick peck on the lips while pressing my business card in his hand. "Call me," I whisper, then climb into my car. As I drive away, I can't help but glance in my rearview mirror to see if he's watching me disappear into the night. Oh yeah, he is.

Over the next couple of months, we spoke on the phone and texted often. Conversations involved local and national news stories, politics, entertainment, religion, and sports. As we grew closer, we shared the difficult losses of our beloved spouses, how we were adjusting to being single, and what we fancied our futures to be. Our conversations began to include what we enjoyed in "private," and texting advanced to sexting along with speculation of pursuing something more. I did not realize it at the time, but he was making love to my mind and soul while my body, especially Precocious Patty, began reacting to the sound of his hypnotizing voice and subtle promise of how he would like to please me. He was *preparing* me for the physicality of lovemaking. A master, indeed.

So, like a slow, sensual dance of intellect the relationship progressed and the conclusion was ultimately reached that yes, the time had come to consummate this cerebral relationship and the planning began for an entire weekend of adventure, exploration, and, hopefully, unbridled passion. Little did I know that our long journey of communication was about to culminate in a physical destination of unbridled joy.

Lesson 28: The journey determines the joy of the final destination.

Chapter 29. Wow, Wow, *Wow*, Joaquin!

The weekend begins early on a Friday afternoon when Joaquin arrives at my door, overnight bag in hand, with a look of intense anticipation mixed with slight apprehension. There I am, barefoot, wearing a simple, low-cut peasant blouse and soft, short skirt. Curly, freshly brushed gray hair (although, like the true gentleman he is, Joaquin calls it "platinum blonde") rests on my shoulders. Mascara highlights my bright blue eyes, and pale pink gloss makes my already full lips look even fuller. My heart is beating so fast I can barely contain my excitement to see where this encounter will take us.

Setting down his bag on the floor, he takes me in his arms and slowly, deliberately, lingeringly kisses just my lips, then deep into my mouth, sucking lightly on my tongue as he withdraws. Now, I've kissed a few men in my life— all right, *way* more than a few—but this kiss quite literally takes my breath away. We step back, eyes wide at the confirmation of undeniable chemistry. With my head resting lightly on his shoulder and one of his arms gently around my waist, we walk to the dining room table.

A light luncheon of chicken salad made personally by yours truly was nestled in wraps of crisp, green Romaine lettuce leaves. Patiently waiting beside the lettuce wraps are ripe, red grape tomatoes. Ice cubes float lazily in flower-etched glasses filled with freshly made cranberry infused iced tea. All carefully choreographed to be eaten without silverware. Fingers only, baby. We inquisitively watch each other lift the lettuce wraps to our mouths, slowly licking our fingers clean of wayward salad. Placing the grape tomatoes between our lips, then sucking them in, chewing slowly. Washing it down with sweet tea from icy glasses. Soon the food is gone and Joaquin stands and silently clears the dishes from the table as I watch. He walks over and takes my trembling hands in his, looks deep in my eyes, and asks if I'm ready. I nod my head yes and lead him down the long hallway to my bedroom.

The stage had been set earlier that day, with shades carefully drawn, a bouquet of fresh summer flowers on the dresser. Lit candles create a romantic glow. Bedding turned down, exposing crisp, clean sheets begging to be mussed. A little nervously we slowly remove each other's clothing, relishing in the sight of our much-anticipated lover's body. Kissing is followed by tentative touching. At long last, we climb on the platform bed and begin the exquisite art of foreplay.

At first, we take turns paying slow, gentle, loving attention to all parts of the other's body. We touch and lick and suck, listening for telltale intakes of breath, moans, and exclamations of joy. Increase or decrease our efforts by the sound of pleasure, feeling the climax come oh so close. Then backing off to increase the anticipation of final release made that much sweeter.

The magnificent sexual tension builds until we can no longer hold back. We've pushed ourselves to the absolute maximum level of pleasure before the final explosion, when he stops suddenly and brings his head up to mine. While his smoldering eyes bore into mine, he once again asks if I am ready. I close my eyes and urgently whisper, "Yes! Please don't stop, Joaquin." He slowly slides inside me, fulfilling that most intimate act of two bodies becoming one. Patty is moaning in ecstasy as I audibly groan, both he and I ultimately screaming out in total and complete fulfillment. With this final act of surrender, I was able to give my entire being to him and was magically transcended beyond this earth to what I call the *Isle of Bliss*. Joaquin is right behind me and we climax simultaneously in a thunderous intertwining of our bodies, minds, and souls.

Totally spent, we collapse, panting heavily, hearts racing and bodies dripping. Even the air is heavy with the smell of musk created by sweaty, salty passion. We hold tightly onto each other, as if our dream lover might simply disappear into thin air. What if it was just an erotic dream? No, it was real. Almost too real to be true but real nonetheless. I cuddle my head in the crook of his shoulder and throw my left leg over his body, just to continue the feeling of his body against mine.

Once our breathing and heart beats return to normal, we quietly discuss the amazing phenomenon of our experience. What it meant to each of us, praising one another, commenting softly on what we especially liked. And what we didn't like. Discussing ways to increase the pleasure "next time." As I reached down to touch him, his body instantly responded and it began all over again.

Two days later, we came up for air feeling drained but completely satisfied in every way—body, mind, and soul.

And that was just the beginning. Each session is a little different with the same glorious outcome. Time truly holds the key to the *Isle of Bliss*. Well, time mixed with variety to spice things up, and the element of surprise that takes *his* breath away when I greet him at the door wearing nothing but a pink-and-black striped corset with thigh-high black seamed stockings, or just a red feather boa tossed around my neck and black high heels on my feet, or fully clothed with a can of whipped cream in my hand and a look of intrigue on my face. Joaquin is full of tricks himself with toys and lotions and DVDs.

And that, my friend, is how you become a truly great lover. It's not just in the act itself, it's in the buildup, the pre- and post-coital whispers and touching and teasing.

I purposely did not describe the personal attributes of this master of lovemaking because it honestly doesn't matter. A great lover can be tall or short, muscled or not, hairy or hairless, well-endowed or barely endowed. It's that he makes love to your entire body, your mind, *and* your soul.

Go ahead, take a break, this was some pretty steamy stuff or read below if you just *have* to know about my extraordinary lover.

Lesson 29: Time holds the key to reaching the Isle of Bliss.

All right, for those dying to know, my extraordinary lover is of average height and build, attractive but not drop-dead gorgeous, balding with white hair on his head, a goatee, and thick dark hair on his chest, belly, and back, impeccably manscaped, strong but not overly muscled, wears glasses, and has big hands and feet that—in his case—correlates to the size of other magnificently fulfilling parts of his body. What truly makes him extraordinary, though, is that his priority is to fully and I mean FULLY satisfy the woman before thinking of his own pleasure. He's man enough to know when he needs help so he's quite happy to use male enhancement supplements to perk up what I've affectionately named Big Boy. He also loves to use a cock ring (a circular rubber or metal ring much like an "o" ring) to help sustain and increase Big Boy's rigidity. No, you cannot borrow him. He's mine, all mine. At least for now.

Chapter 30. Master and Commander

One of the most important lessons I have learned in the game of life is that I can either accept the hand it's dealt me or fold and draw new cards. This grand and glorious adventure we call life is strewn with both easy and complex situations that can improve, stagnate, or degrade our journey. It is up to each of us to look deep inside ourselves and make the needed changes that will give us the life we *deserve*.

Throughout my teenage years, I ended my evening prayers asking God to challenge me in whatever way He chose... "but please, please I beg of you Heavenly Father, please don't do anything to disfigure my face or hinder my intellect." So when I got pregnant out of wedlock and began having seizures at age eighteen, I was certain I was being punished for my false pride and arrogance. Too ashamed to speak to my parents, minister, or even my young husband, I hid my shame and begged God for forgiveness. Seven long years of secretly seeing doctors and specialists for second and third opinions, suffering through test after test, taking tranquilizers and muscle relaxants, and still nothing helped. The seizures continued. They were strange—I felt as if my brain *s-l-o-w-l-y* ceased to function, followed by hallucinations that my thoughts were being said aloud on the television or radio. Next came total loss of energy, garbled speech, throat contractions, and dilated pupils. To avoid completely collapsing I would sink to the floor, laying down anything I was holding beside me there, even my precious babies. Each episode was more terrifying than the last, leaving me horribly frightened and totally exhausted.

After experiencing thirteen seizures in one day, I packed an overnight bag, took my sons to my mother's home, drove the long trip across town to our family doctor, and sat in his office, declaring that I could not live with the uncertainty of these "spells," as I called them, and was not leaving until an answer was found to relieve my symptoms. He bowed his gray head, lines on his face seeming to deepen as I watched, almost seeing his mind whirling, trying to come up with an answer that totally and completely eluded him. After a long pause, this dear sweet man, who had become a friend through our long torturous journey of attempted discovery, promised to move heaven and earth to help me. After another long pause, he phoned a friend, one of the top neurologists in Los Angeles, and arranged an emergency office visit for me that same day. Ignoring my fear of having another spell, I immediately drove to his office.

After another battery of tests, I was diagnosed with psychomotor epilepsy. I was told an overload of electrical activity was causing my brain to trigger the release of energy and the brain to temporarily malfunction. Two anti-seizure medications were prescribed and, after a few weeks, the seizures slowed down to twice a month or so. My family doctor regretfully explained that I would never be able to hold a full-time job or even a part-time job, because stress was one of the major seizure triggers. There were other triggers as well, like becoming too hungry, too tired, too emotional, and so on. I was instructed to live an unemotional life free of stress. Really? With two small sons and barely enough money to pay the bills on my husband's salary? Good luck with *that*.

I knew there was only one possible reason for this shameful diagnosis. God was punishing me by giving me a disease of the brain. Of all things, *my brain* was tainted! Being devastated far beyond the depth of my soul, I stayed home for two years, certain that an invisible "E" for epilepsy had been burnt into my forehead, alerting every person on the planet of my diagnosis and humiliation.

One day, my mother came over and begged me to return to a normal life. I sobbed while explaining to her I could never return to a normal life; it was God's punishment for my arrogance as a teenager. My dear sweet mother, my rock, took me in her arms and assured me that it was not God's intention to punish, but for each of us to *learn* from our trials and tribulations.

The relief I felt was instant and I can never thank my mother enough for helping me wade through the worst dilemma of my life. With her help, I slowly resumed a normal life, and began part-time work when my boys were in school. After my divorce, I held a full-time job as an executive assistant at a large company, along with two part-time jobs as a bookkeeper for a small homeowners association and as a home party dealer.

Doctors know only so much. That's why medicine is called a practice. So don't believe anyone who tells you differently, that you are limited in what you can do. Prove them wrong. Like I did and continue to do.

Lesson 30: I am, you are, we all are the masters and commanders of our own destinies.

Chapter 31. Reawakening Jason

One gorgeous spring night, I met a girlfriend at a local casino lounge for a couple of drinks and to dance to '60s tunes by a live band. It felt as though we were reliving the '60s instead of being *in* our 60s and, personally, I was feeling no pain when I walked up to the bar to order *another* glass of wine (don't judge). Earlier that night, I had enjoyed chatting with Gabriel, a personable young man playing video poker at the bar. Fortyish, dark hair, nice build, Garth Brooks t-shirt with jeans and work boots, you know the type, probably married, dreading going home to a bitchy wife. Definitely harmless.

Gabriel had been sitting at the bar a little too long and was trying to relieve his aching, stiff muscles by hunching his shoulders and then flexing his nicely muscled arms. While waiting to get the bartender's attention, I absent-mindedly reached over and began massaging his neck and shoulders, almost instantly feeling the tension melt away. He asked me how I knew he needed a massage. I told him I was a widow and had given my husband many massages and actually kind of missed it. He smiled gratefully, thanked me, and paid for my drink. Nice.

So naturally, the next time I needed a refill, I squeezed between Gabriel and a new guy sitting next to him. While waiting on the very slow bartender I once again massaged Gabriel's neck and, with the other hand, rubbed the new guy's neck as well. It was a Saturday night and I was bored, so why not? New Guy was pleasantly surprised and very grateful for the small gesture. Next thing I know, New Guy sticks out his hand and says, "Why, thank you for that. My name is Jason. What's yours?" I was impressed with such an unexpected gesture—most guys will introduce themselves but not with the friendly handshake thing. This could be interesting.

As the evening wore on, I came back again and again for fresh drinks (occasionally just *water*, okay?). Jason was still sitting there, always smiling, and we began to engage in very enjoyable conversation. Soon I accepted his offer to sit next to him. It turned out he was twenty years my junior but what the heck, I wasn't going to marry the kid, just talk to him. His kind eyes crinkled when he laughed while he nervously adjusted his glasses and tucked his longish blonde hair behind his ears. His quick wit made for very interesting banter as we touched on many topics and, as the booze flowed and the night grew late, we began discussing our romantic interests. The easy rapport led to revealing some extremely intimate information about ourselves.

To my amazement, this very attractive young man had not been with a woman for over six years. Jason explained he'd literally caught his ex-wife in bed with a very well-endowed lover and that alone caused serious doubts about his masculinity. But she, the guilty one, couldn't leave it at that. Oh no, she threw it in his face and, after screaming insult after insult, her parting words were, "I faked it, you sorry son of a bitch! Your member is so small you could *never* please any woman with that tiny little *thing*!" Her words were like a knife thrust into his heart, leaving him a shell of his former confident self. Since then he had not dared to date, for fear of ridicule.

What that woman did to him is the cruelest thing one person can do to another. To ridicule a person's sexuality, indeed their ability to please the opposite sex, is totally reprehensible. I forgot Precocious Patty was listening silently to Jason's tale of woe. When the story ended, she emphatically demanded that we take him home with us just to build up his self-esteem. This was purely an act of kindness. Patty begged, pleaded, and cajoled, reminding me that after my divorce I had felt the same way, because I'd been replaced by a much younger woman. That I'd felt used, abused, and discarded until a young man took pity on me and reaffirmed my desirability. Still, despite Patty's pleadings, I remained adamant that I wanted no part of "fixing" this man's problems. Sounded like way too much work to me.

The evening ended with a vague agreement to perhaps meet for a drink the following weekend. As I started to turn away, he touched my arm and said, "Wait, let me give you my phone number in case you'd like to talk or something." He sent his number from his cell phone to mine and our friendship began.

Jason was in the middle of a long-distance online relationship with a young lady in California he'd never had the courage to meet. I had been in a six-month exclusive relationship with my Don Juan Joaquin, who'd recently announced we should see others. That there was a lovely woman ten years his senior that he would like to pursue. To feel the thrill of the chase, as he put it. And that I should do the same. Find someone to fill my time and invite into my bed when he was off with his next conquest. Fine. With the timing of this announcement, young Jason seemed like the perfect solution to Joaquin's absence in my life. It'd be a challenge, but I'm never one to shy away from a challenge.

Throughout the next week, Jason and I texted and sexted teasingly until a dilemma arose. Should we risk complicating our existing relationships by having a quiet affair, or walk away from one another? The chemistry between us was utterly and totally undeniable and we feared if we met in person again, the temptation would be too strong to resist. To see each other again or not, that was the question.

Precocious Patty chattered all week about Jason. His cherubic face, fascinating eyes—one blue, one hazel—his soft blond hair, his muscular body, the obvious bulge in his jeans when we last parted company. Throughout the next couple of weeks Jason texted, heart-wrenchingly sharing what he felt were his shortcomings (pardon the pun) and what he needed help overcoming, namely his lack of experience as a lover. Patty really, *really* wanted to help him and, as usual, ultimately got her way. I was certain my abundance of experience could help him overcome any sexual difficulties and insecurities. I encouraged him to let me help him. We agreed to meet at his apartment the following Saturday night for his first lesson from Precocious Patty, the Sex Counselor.

Patty and I took the entire day to prepare for this first of what would be many intimate encounters, by scrubbing and lotioning ourselves from head to toe. Washing, drying, and styling my platinum hair. Meticulously painting my fingernails and toenails a sweet, soft pink. After carefully applying my makeup I dabbed my oh-so-appropriately-named cologne, *Pleasures*, behind my ears, between my breasts, and just below my belly button. I pulled on tight, faded denim jeans, a soft pink V-neck sweater that coquettishly revealed the swell of my bosom, and nervously made the ten-minute drive to his place.

Jason was the gentleman I hoped he would be, by meeting me outside his apartment and guiding me to a nearby parking space. He opened my car door, took my hand, and as I climbed out, I found myself being gently drawn into his arms as he whispered softly into my ear, "I feel like I'm dreaming. Is this really happening?"

His apartment was immaculate, with ivory walls, a masculine brown sofa, and matching loveseat embellished with gold studs. A flat-screen T.V. over the natural gas fireplace completed the living room. His well-stocked kitchen included a charming, standing wine opener and a refrigerator stocked with chilled bottles of beer and white wine. A bottle of red wine stood on the counter. I noticed an open bottle of beer on the counter—his. When asked if I'd like a drink, I nodded toward the beer and said, "I'd like one like yours, no glass." I wanted him to see the way I drank from the long neck of the bottle. It got the reaction I'd hoped for—his utter and complete attention to my every move created tangible anticipation of what was about to unfold.

We both knew why I was there. We drank our beers and chatted nervously for a while. When I set my drink down and walked over to gaze out the living room picture window, Jason did the same, coming up behind me and folding me into his arms. I heard his breath catch in his throat when I pressed my body back into his. Huskily, he asked if I'd like a tour of the rest of the apartment. Patty was, by this time, urging me, *Get on with it for crying out loud*, whispering to me that she could feel the excitement building in his shorts, and it would be *horrifically* unjust to force him to wait any longer for that which he so desperately longed for, namely her. I accepted his offer for the tour.

Gently taking my hand into his, Jason guided me to a small bedroom furnished with a twin bed, tiny white dresser, and large wooden toy chest, explaining the room was for occasional visits by his young daughter. I sighed in relief that this was *not* his room and we slowly walked down the hallway to a second bedroom, large and masculine, with a sliding glass door leading to a lovely balcony overlooking the complex. A beautifully waxed and polished oak dresser stood against one wall, its matching nightstand complete with a charming old school LED alarm clock against the other wall. A modern, silver floor lamp cast a soft, warm glow on the room's magnificent centerpiece—a huge California king bed, complete with passionately red satin sheets peeking out from under a velvety smoke-gray bedspread that seemed to summon us to indulge in its exquisiteness.

We engaged in a long, slow, sensual kiss until I pulled away and murmured, "Are you sure this is what you want?" After gazing deeply into my eyes, he slowly smiled, winked. and then whispered, "Oh yes, I am more than ready. I've been waiting for this moment for over six years."

I asked him to dim the lights and get comfortable while I used the master bathroom. After removing most of my clothing, I opened the door to find Jason waiting nervously at the foot of the bed, wearing nothing but pale blue and black checkered boxer shorts. He nearly fainted when he saw me stripped down to my lacy black and pink bra and matching panties.

I approached Jason, then turned away and asked him to help finish undressing me. Indeed, he did. He fumbled while attempting to undo my bra, finally managing to release all four hooks, then whistled softly as I slowly turned toward him, shrugging my shoulders to let my bra fall to the floor. Before I knew it, my panties were off and, with a flick of his wrist, Jason slingshot them across the room, laughing raucously and admitting he'd wanted to do that his whole life. I shook my head and giggled gleefully as I realized what a man-child this forty-nine-year-old still was. Patty agreed and virtually shouted, *Let's get on with it already*!

And so, Lovemaking 101 began. Now, you have to realize I was expecting a barely endowed, clumsy, inexperienced boy in a man's body. But to my utter delight Jason was of average size, with a delightful curve that touched my magical G-spot on every single stroke. And stroke it he did. He dove right in with the enthusiasm of a teenager trying all the things he had only dreamed of.

After our first session left my heart pounding and nerves tingling, Jason confessed that although he had not actually made love to a woman in six years he had watched and studied a great deal of online self-help videos and pornography, and that I was the first woman he tried any of it on. Wow! What he learned from those videos was astonishing to say the least. His technique was flawless from first touch to Patty's explosive multiple orgasms. In addition to his torrid sensuality he was an exceptionally considerate lover, concentrating on *my needs* first. Taking me to heights of ecstasy I suspect have rarely been felt by any woman. Then I satisfied his needs. First the sucking and licking of his most erogenous zones, then culminating in my slowly lowering myself onto his waiting body, penetrating slowly at first, then progressively faster until the steady pounding took him past the point of no return, explosively releasing everything he had held back for so long. With his legs quivering and heart pounding, our first session was over.

Rolling off, I took Jason in my arms, placing his head on my chest until his ragged breath calmed enough for him to speak. He thanked me profusely for the very best night of his entire life. Then he nervously asked if he was as bad a lover as his wife claimed.

Jason's question took me by surprise, since I am certainly not a silent lover but rather more of a moaner and groaner and occasional screamer. Patty reminded me to proceed cautiously with my assessment because he was really, really good and we both wanted his "lessons" to continue for purely selfish reasons. So, after gathering my thoughts, I told him his size definitely was *not* wanting, in fact he might be a little on the generous side and his lovemaking style had definite possibilities. This ensured we would enjoy future "lovemaking lessons," although I'm not sure which one of us was doing the teaching.

Jason and I were able to keep our mostly sexual relationship separate from the emotional relationships with our significant others, resulting in each session creating an almost dream-like state that was extremely powerful but not quite real. The severe emotional damage inflicted by one cruel and insensitive woman was slowly replaced by the self-esteem he so richly deserved.

Lesson 31: Words can cut deeper than any knife ever can.

Chapter 32. Jason Has His Eyes Opened

Building up Jason's confidence as a man was next on my lesson planner. Although he was a trained professional in his field and highly accomplished in martial arts, he was timid in personal relationships, rarely looking directly at women or speaking to them. Until I came along. Whenever we were in public, I coached him on who was looking at him and what their glances and comments meant. If a woman walks by making direct eye contact, she is most likely available. Speak up, introduce yourself. Make small talk. If a woman makes physical contact, such as placing her hand on your arm, she'd like you to ask her to sit next to you or perhaps have a dance. If she speaks to you first *and* makes physical contact, she is definitely interested in you as a man, perhaps even a potential *lover*.

In just a few days after this lesson, Jason texted, asking me why women were suddenly coming on to him. "Jason, you're just finally noticing them," I texted back. "Really? Me?" he asked. And then he really started paying attention. He told me about a beautiful young neighbor who saw him in the parking lot walked over to say hello and made small talk. "Diana, she made me feel like a million bucks. Maybe I am a little attractive," he said. "Jason," I assured him, "you are a sexy, handsome man. You just didn't believe it before."

And so, it continues. Walks with his boxer/pit bull mix dog Twilight became the highlight of each morning and evening. Now he notices that the tiny, curvy blonde with the Yorkshire puppy always runs to catch up to him and ask him about his day. The redhead jogging with her German shepherd every morning, who crosses the road to say hello to him and Twilight. The scatter-brained brunette at work swooping in while he's filling up his giant to-go mug at the coffee bar, who makes it clear she is definitely interested in him.

Jason panicked a little when I suggested he ask for their phone numbers. No, no, he's not ready to go any further just yet, he said, he needs a little more time, then feels guilty. He's still in contact with his long-time, long-distance online girlfriend who he someday hopes to meet in person. And he needs more lovemaking lessons from me. *Woo-hoo*, screams Patty after waking up from a weeklong Jason-less coma. *Ask him if we can see him tonight please, please, please,* she begs. She needs to see him and his friends, Dicky and Licky. Dicky and Licky? I ask Patty. *You know who I'm talking about.* I totally know who they are. Yes, let's invite Dicky and Licky to party.

His confidence continued to grow until he was ready to fly the coop, to leave the nest, to let Dicky and Licky strike out on their own. At our last session Jason tearfully thanked me from the bottom of his heart for teaching him about women and allowing him to practice until he was as perfect a lover as I have ever known. In fact, Jason's self-confidence had improved to near cockiness (pun intended)

160

although I must admit I'd rather see a man a little on the cocky side than doubting his worth as a lover. Score one for Precocious Patty talking me into giving him a chance.

Patty held a wake for Dicky and Licky and refused to come out to play for a good week but we ain't done yet. Age is just a number. It won't take long to find our next project. Heck, maybe the next guy will tame us to the point that Patty and I will be content to spend Saturday night on the sofa, watching movies, and eating popcorn.

Stop laughing. It could happen.

Lesson 32: Practice does make perfect.

Chapter 33. What Son No. 1 and Eric Idle Both Know

Always having been a positive-minded person—you know, the kind who sees the glass as half full instead of half empty—my highly optimistic attitude simply does not hold a candle to my oldest son's. Even as a child bad luck seemed to follow Robbie (who became Bob at sixteen and too grown up for a "baby name") around like a lost puppy. He was the kid who would fall in the mud puddle all the other children managed to avoid, the one to inevitably get a nose bleed during the class play, to trip on his way to first base in T-ball, and have his finger painting artwork fall off the wall during open house at school. In other words, if anything could possibly go wrong, it did. Even his grandma Wanda started calling him Charlie Brown because of his constant bad luck.

Except he didn't see it that way at all. That child always found the bright side of any situation. To him, falling in the mud was actually kind of cool because it was fun watching the mud dry on his pants. The nosebleed brought a bit of drama to the play and that's why, he was pretty sure, his class won first place in the county for Best Play. Tripping on his way to first base distracted the outfielder so much he missed the ball because he was laughing so hard and it allowed the winning run to score. The teacher told the class that the finger painting falling off the wall during open house lightened the otherwise somber mood and everyone got a good laugh out of it.

Nature or nurture? As much as I would love to claim that nurture had anything to do with his attitude, I think nature was responsible. Robbie was born a happy baby, and was so happy-go-lucky that as a kindergartener his elementary school principal awarded him a certificate for having the *"The Smilingest Smile I Have Ever Seen."* And that pretty much sums it up.

For his thirteenth birthday, my sister Wilma sadly told Robbie she had been hoping to take him and his cousins miniature golfing but just couldn't afford it this year. "That's okay, Auntie," he told her, grinning from ear to ear. "We haven't had a day alone together for a really long time." And so they had their day together, and she had just enough money to play one round of miniature golf (which of course he won like he always did), two dollars in quarters for video games, one hot dog each and one drink to share, making it, according to him, "The bestest birthday anyone could ever ask for!" He wasn't at all disappointed that his cousins couldn't come.

After my divorce, when I was terrified I wouldn't be able to pay the bills, Robbie said not to worry, something would come through for me, and it did. I got a job that allowed us to squeak by at first, and that later more than covered the bills plus a nice 401k that allowed me to take an early retirement. When his brother Eddy was nearly killed in a terrible accident, Robbie told me everything would be okay, that it was in God's hands, not mine. And he was right, all my worrying did not add up to a hill of beans but prayer did, and Eddy survived with just a broken leg and a few cuts and bruises.

When the pipes broke under our triple-wide trailer and we had to go without water *for a month* while I saved money to get it fixed, was he worried? Nope. He helped make it an adventure by coming up with solutions for all our needs. We took early morning hot showers in our swimsuits at the trailer park's outdoor shower down by the swimming pool. He trudged water by the bucketfuls from the faucet at the empty trailer pad next door to flush our toilets and heat on the stove to wash dishes. He taught me the fun of people watching during the tedious chore of doing our laundry at the local laundromat. Indeed, Robbie made it seem like an adventure instead of a disaster.

When my husband, Louie, passed away, Robbie, now Bob, reminded me that his stepdad was finally out of pain forever and it was true. Louie had been hiding the misery of ill health for over twenty years during which surgeons had "gutted him like a tuna" (Louie's words, not mine) to remove his gall bladder filled with over one hundred stones. Later he had a heart attack and had to have a stent placed in his heart. His favorite foods were taken away when he was placed on a very strict diet, at first for Type II diabetes, with more restrictions later when he was diagnosed with end-stage kidney disease. He even had to give up his beloved Corona beer *forever* when he went through treatment for Hepatitis C. His muscles were wasting, he was unsteady on his feet, his hair was thinning, his vision impaired. But I didn't care, I had wanted him to stay alive for *me*. Because *I* needed him. Bob helped me picture Louie in heaven, eating anything he wanted, washing it down with a beer, shooting pool with all his friends who had gone on before him, and being our very own, personal guardian angel. "Mom, he's happy now. He's out of pain. We were lucky we had him as long as we did," Bob said, followed by that beautiful smile of his, a wink, and a nod. And he was right. Like always. He steered me away from the dark side so I could see the bright side again.

I talked to my son about writing this chapter and here's what he had to say. "That's me, Mom. I know everything works out for the best. We always get through the tough times and wind up stronger because of it."

I'm pretty sure his attitude is a tad magical, too. For years his wife, Shannon, talked ceaselessly about renovating their kitchen. I knew beyond a doubt they would *never* have the money to do it and thought to myself what a silly, unachievable, time-wasting dream she had. Then one day they inherited enough money to renovate the kitchen. Shows how much I know, right?

Bob insisted on doing much of the renovation himself in order to save loads of money. Oh Lord, my Charlie Brown was taking on a huge project with so many possibilities for failure! There I went again, looking on the dark side. Turns out that even Charlie Browns are wise enough to hire plumbers and electricians to do the hard stuff, and Bob's positive attitude resulted in a beautiful new kitchen. He even made it fun for the whole family when his wife insisted he let their youngest wield a sledgehammer to knock down one of the walls. Yes, it took a little longer than if he had done it by himself but those are memories that will remain with that kid forever. That and to be just like Dad—

to always look on the bright side of life. With a smile, a wink, and a nod.

Now I know what looking at the dark side does. Absolutely nothing. Except make you miserable and sad. Looking on the bright side, well, it can be and often is, downright *magical.*

Lesson 33: The dark side of life is ugly. So listen to and always remember, "Always Look On the Bright Side of Life."

Chapter 34. One Final Lesson.
from Son No. 2

A child dreams of being a cowboy, ballerina, doctor, lawyer, veterinarian, astronaut, athlete, rock star, actor, mommy, daddy. I dreamed of being a writer, and wrote stories from when I was a child through my teens. As an adult I wrote local newspaper columns, was the editor of a small newsletter for many years, and won local, state, and national awards for reports and articles. I always wanted to write a book. I started a few self-help books but lost interest in writing them (not very helpful, was I?). Then I was inspired to write again when I heard from my youngest son, Eddy, that he was making his life-long dream a reality.

Even as a very young boy, he loved the sound of fire engine and police car sirens. It meant someone or something was in peril and, like super heroes, the first responders were on their way to save the day! As a young man, he learned first-hand the importance of these trained professionals when he was involved in a terrible auto accident a few weeks after turning sixteen. Firefighters used jaws-of-life to remove two unconscious, broken, and bleeding bodies from the twisted metal of his Honda Civic. Shortly after the ambulance reached the hospital, I got the phone call every parent dreads, "Your son has been injured. He's still alive. Get here as fast as you can."

Excitedly on their way to an Angels baseball game in Anaheim, Eddy, his cousin Ted, the cousin's neighbor, Frank, and the neighbor's son, Frankie, had stopped to pick up a quick dinner of burgers, fries, and sodas before getting on the freeway. What began as a fun outing soon turned into a nightmare. The cars on the eastbound 91 freeway began to slow, then suddenly stopped while my son was checking his blind spot to change lanes. His passengers screamed for him to stop but by the time he looked up the Civic had smashed into a van filled with a Mom, Dad, and kids. Guardian angels must have been hovering nearby that day because, after the stench of the tires' burning rubber and the sound of crunching metal had subsided, the family in the van was uninjured. Eddy and Frank were not so lucky. They lay in the front bucket seats, bleeding and unconscious. Ted and Frankie, the two hysterical fourteen-year-old boys, were trapped in the back seat, terrified that their cousin and father's motionless bodies meant they were dead.

Two motorcyclists, Jim and John, who were traveling behind the accident managed to avoid being involved, maneuvering around the twisted metal of the crumpled cars. They stopped and began administering first aid. They assured the sobbing boys in the back that they would get them out of the car as soon as they attended to the injured. Jim wrapped my son's badly bleeding head—caused by the windshield slicing off most of his scalp—in his own t-shirt. John applied pressure to a badly bleeding artery while Jim removed his belt, positioned it, and then tightened it above the open, exposed flesh of Eddy's badly cut knee. The men then gently swaddled Frank's mangled forearm in one of their jackets before finally pulling the frightened, weeping teenagers out through the hatchback window.

Jim and John, the motorcyclists, were off-duty firefighters at a nearby oil refinery. They recognized two of the passengers, Frank and Frankie, as a co-worker and his son. After filling the paramedics in on the aid they had administered and assessing the situation, they determined it was best to remove the frightened boys from the ghastly scene, so they placed their helmets on Ted and Frankie, loaded them on the backs of their motorcycles, and kindly drove the boys to their nearby homes. The teenagers were beyond elated when they received the call that their cousin and dad *were* still alive, albeit severely injured, and had arrived safely at the hospital. Then and only then did Ted and Frankie allow their moms to take them to the emergency room for evaluation. The nurses treated them for shallow cuts and vacuumed the broken windshield glass from their hair.

After being extricated from the car, Eddy and Frank were transported by ambulance to the nearest emergency room and treated for multiple injuries. Several surgeries and very long recovery periods later they were nearly as good as new, mostly because of two off-duty firefighters who selflessly administered first aid at the scene of the accident.

First responders were elevated to near god-like status in Eddy's mind after that fateful day. It prompted him to take fire science courses at a community college, with the full intention of becoming a firefighter. But when he completed the courses he decided to go in a different direction and began a career in the food industry. He fell in love, got married, and he and his wife eventually bought a pizza franchise. They worked day and night to succeed, selling the franchise after a few years to open what would become an award-winning sushi restaurant. When the economy took a downturn, they sold the restaurant and moved to the east coast where they began separate, different careers. Eddy joined a software company; his wife, Merrie, became a personal chef.

Although financially and professionally successful, Eddy still secretly yearned to be a firefighter. Did he beat himself up for not becoming one when he was young? Nope. Instead, he took steps to make that dream a reality. At the age of forty-eight he passed the physical and written exams and was suddenly a real-life, honest-to-goodness small town volunteer firefighter, and now is enjoying the most rewarding time of his life.

In just a few months of going out on calls, he has assisted in the transportation of infants, children, and adults with life-threatening medical conditions to Medevac helicopters, where they were taken to hospitals equipped to handle their conditions. Eddy's guided powerful fire hoses with thousands of gallons of water arching upward to extinguish flames devouring homes while families helplessly watched. He's escorted countless eager school children through his firehouse, always watching for that glint of purpose and excitement he knew was present in his own eyes at their age.

Saving lives and fighting fires with the full support of his wife and sons, while making a good living at his full-time job, has made his life truly a dream come true. As a bonus, he may even be helping his oldest son, Bryce, a very talented young photographer, with his own dreams, when the seventeen-year-old was appointed the fire station's official photographer.

It's never too late to pursue your dreams no matter how old you are or how impossible they may seem. The only thing holding us back is ourselves. Our lack of purpose, drive, and inspiration. People of all ages run marathons and compete as athletes, or take to the stage to compete as singers and dancers on reality shows. So why not you? You just have to want it badly enough and then simply *do it*. My son at long last became a firefighter. At age sixty-nine, I've now written a book. Just as we always wanted to.

Lesson 34: Never, ever, ever give up on your dreams.

Afterword

There are good men *and* bad men out there. I have loved and learned from both. The most important lesson I learned is that a man should be judged by the way he makes *you feel*, not by the way he looks, the size of his bank account, his hands, or his feet.

Perhaps now you understand why I tend to shy away from rich, powerful men who treat women like trophies on their arms or the prize in a box of Cracker Jacks, neither of which I am content to be. The blue-collar worker—now, *he* knows how to treat me. I'm the queen of his universe. A goddess sent him from above. So give me your tired, your poor (not *too* poor though), your naturally muscled, hard-working men. Please.

As for you, my dear readers, go forth and strive to make your mate, your partner, your lover, your spouse, your child feel like the most remarkable person on the planet, and they will respond ten-fold. If you have not as yet found that absolute match, that perfect person, your soul mate (I know it seems cliché but believe me, soul mates *do* exist; I know, I found mine), perhaps my lessons will help you find him or her before your time on this amazing earth runs out.

But most importantly, be good to yourself.

Look on the bright side.

Love like there is no tomorrow.

Make your dream a reality.

Write that book.

Run that marathon.

Eat that cake. (That was for me, there's some in the fridge).

Acknowledgements

First and foremost, I would like to thank each and every person that has ever walked into, and sometimes, out of my life. All of us influence one another in some way or another. Some of you will see yourselves in my book while others may not. But you all influenced me.

Thank you to all the kids who attended Walteria Elementary School in Torrance, California, from 1952–1962, for never once making me feel ashamed of my oh-so-round, roly-poly body. Not even so much as one single classmate ever called me fatso or pushed me down or made fun of me. At least not to my face, and that's all I care about.

A shout-out to my Typing I and II and Stenography I and II (Google it if you've never heard of either one) teacher, Mr. Carlson, at South High School in Torrance for nominating me as Best Business Student of the Senior Class of 1965–1966. I still have that little plaque that validates to this day that I would be an asset to the business world.

To Sylvia and Jon Boyd and their daughters, Leslie and Lorna, for having seen past the stigma of "epileptic" and giving me a chance to become a successful dealer and manager in their Tupperware Home Parties distributorship, Humming Boyd Sales of Inglewood, California.

To the late Larry Poland for giving me a chance to re-enter the professional world after my divorce, by hiring me as his secretary at FujiFilm in Cypress, California. To all my Fuji friends—Cheryl, Donna Rae, Sandra, Mark, Alan, Christy, Dave, Steve, Harold (Anastacio), and dozens and dozens more—you all helped me see my potential and achieve my goals.

To my family—my mom, Wanda; Dad, Frank Howe; and sisters, Linda and Wilma and brother-in-law Rick. We had a wonderful life together, and Linda and Wilma, thank you for helping me remember childhood incidents that had become a little fuzzy in my own brain. To my two husbands, first Bob (for eighteen years) and then the late Louie (for twenty-six) for loving me and helping me become the person I am today.

To my sons, Bob Jr. and Ed, who have kept me anchored to this world since the day they were born. Who loved me unconditionally as children and still do to this day. Who were what gave me a reason to keep on when I felt too miserable to face the light of another day. To their families, who have continued the same loving tradition of my sons, and from whom I have learned so much—Bob's wife Shannon (of 25 years) and their children, Amanda, Noah, and Timothy; Ed's wife Merrie (of 21 years) and their sons, Bryce and Charlie. Thank you for your constant support, especially this past year as I have devoted much of my time writing and re-writing and re-re-writing.

To my dear friends Judy and Linda. You agreed to read the first, faltering chapters and enthusiastically encouraged me to pursue my writing. To my American Legion, American Legion Auxiliary, and VFW Auxiliary friends for their constant reassurance that I could do this.

To my roommates, Daniel and Debbie, for putting up with my writer's temperament and occasional tantrums when the words just would not come.

To Shirley Sander's Page Turner's Book Club members for their consistent support and especially to author and Page Turner member, My Haley, who has become a dear friend and wonderful mentor for her invaluable suggestions, assistance and encouragement. Finally to my editor Paula Stahel, for making a reality of my dream of sharing with the world some of the lessons I have learned.